You Can Build It

Book 1

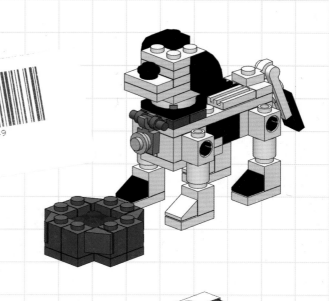

Table of Contents

Sculpture:
Models that are in a unique scale outside of minifigure scale, such as Miniland scale and life-scale.

Minifigure Scale
Models that are in scale with LEGO minifigures.

Micro or Mini Scale
Models that are scaled to either a person being one brick, or one brick and one plate, in height.

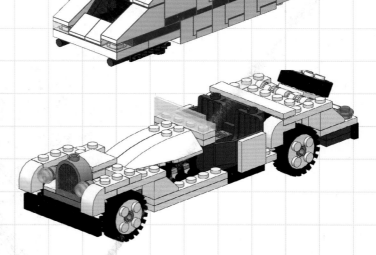

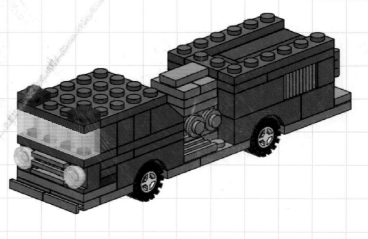

You Can Build It! Book 1

One Very Tired Author, Layout Artist, Designer and Writer: Joe Meno

Publisher and Proofreader: John Morrow

Contributors: Geoff Gray, Christopher Deck, Jason Railton, Didier Enjary.

BrickJournal and its staff would like to thank the LDraw community for the software it makes available to the community, which we use for making all of the instructions and renderings in this magazine. We would especially like to thank Kevin Clague for his continued upgrades of the LPub tool that is a part of the LDraw suite. For more information, please visit *http://www.ldraw.org*.

Some of the content in *You Can Build It, Book 1* has been previously printed in *BrickJournal* Magazine

Published by:

TwoMorrows Publishing
10407 Bedfordtown Drive
Raleigh, NC 27614
www.twomorrows.com
e-mail: store@twomorrowspubs.com

First Printing: January 2012
Printed in China
ISBN: 978-1-60549-035-9

Trademarks and Copyrights:

Dedication

You know, none of what has happened to me would have happened if I didn't get that first LEGO set, so this is dedicated to my parents, who got me my first sets.

And none of this would have happened if I didn't start posting on LUGNET, so thanks Todd and Suz for starting that site. Many things have changed, but the beginning for me was there.

And none of this would have happened if I didn't go to BrickFest way back in 2002 and meet many of the friends that I still have today: Mike and Erica Huffman, Felix Greco, Scott Lyttle, Chris Giddens, Mark Sandlin, and Tony Perez.

And none of this would have happened if I hadn't made *BrickJournal* with Geoff Gray, Jim Foulds, and Allan Bedford.

And none of this would have happened if the LEGO Group hadn't reached out to get *BrickJournal* to print, thanks to Tormod Askildsen and Paal Smith-Meyer.

And none of this would have happened if John Morrow hadn't offered to be *BrickJournal's* publisher. Thanks John.

And thank you for reading this far... now go build!

Joe Meno

Glossary

AFOL (Adult Fan of LEGO)
NLSO (Non-LEGO Significant Other)
MOC (My Own Creation)
TLG (The LEGO Group)
BURP (Big Ugly Rock Piece)
LURP (Little Ugly Rock Piece)
POOP (Pieces—that can be or should be made—Of Other Pieces)
SNOT (Studs Not on Top)
LUG (LEGO Users Group)
LTC (LEGO Train Club)

Welcome...

...to the first volume of the *You Can Build It* series of books. Originally, these were going to be simply compilations of the instructions from *BrickJournal* magazine, but the series changed as it was being designed.

The book became a set of instructions that went up in levels, from beginner to intermediate to expert. *BrickJournal*'s instructions were for beginner to intermediate builders interested in building new things. These books are a more focused document to show building.

One thing that is a common thread in these models is that they use mostly common parts, so hopefully you will have many of the parts needed for a model already in the sets you have bought. If not, the part lists have the information you need to find any missing parts online. If you want a complete list of the parts used in this book, you can download it at: *http://www.twomorrows.com/media/YouCanBuildIt1List.pdf*

If you don't have internet access and want a hardcopy of the list, send a self-addressed stamped envelope to:

You Can Build It Parts List
TwoMorrows Publishing
10407 Bedfordtown Drive
Raleigh, NC 27614

"Finding Parts" is the first section of this book. Searching for the right part can be a long, painful process. Hopefully the guide in the next few pages will make it a little easier for you.

Most of the models here use basic building techniques, so this is a good start into LEGO building. The techniques shown in the models are a good look at how you can make a model a certain shape, or function a certain way. The scales of the models are a variety, so you have a chance to build an assortment of items, from an attack helicopter to a floral arrangement.

When it became apparent that the book would have to have models of a specific skill level, I took a look at my creation library. I have built LEGO models for over ten years, and still have some of my beginning models, which are included here.

Other contributors include people from all around — Christopher Deck from Germany, Jason Railton from England, Didier Enjary from France, and Geoff Gray from the US. Later editions will have more builders included, as models get more complex.

Models are arranged in categories; Sculpture (where you will see building techniques), Minifigure scale (if you want to build something for your LEGO figures) and Micro scale, so start where you want to and start building!

Don't have all the parts in your collection to build the sets shown in this book? You can download a complete parts list in PDF form, with links to find the ones you need online. Just go to this link:

http://www.twomorrows.com/media/YouCanBuildIt1List.pdf

Finding and Ordering Parts

LEGO building, like any building, requires resources. The typical LEGO builder has at least a few thousand parts on hand to build. While that sounds like a large number, it isn't hard to gather that many parts. What is hard is getting the *right* parts.

There are a few ways to find parts here. I'm going to show you where you can find parts.

The LEGO Group

The obvious way to get parts is to go to either a LEGO Brand Retail Store or online at www.lego.com.

At the LEGO stores, there will be a wall of bricks and other parts that you can purchase by the cup. It's called Pick-A-Brick, and is the quickest way to get a large number of parts. The catch is that they have a limited selection.

Online, you can go to www.brickbuildr.com or more precisely, http://ipab.brickbuildr.com/ and see Pick-A-Brick listings for most LEGO stores. Keep in mind, though, that the listings may not always be up to date.

The LEGO website also has a Pick-A-Brick. Use the keywords Pick a Brick to find the page. Here you can buy by single piece. but know what part you want, as the parts library has more than a few categories.

The website sells parts individually, so buying can become expensive. However, the parts ordered are new from the factory.

The LEGO Group's webpage—use the search box at the top to find Pick a Brick

Bricklink

If you are looking for a rare part or an element that has been out of production—like, say, a motor for a monorail set—you will have to go to Bricklink (www.bricklink.com).

Bricklink is a worldwide network of third-party LEGO vendors. What's nice about the site is that the members sell sets and parts from new and old LEGO sets. For builders, this site has become an important resource for part selection and purchasing.

As mentioned before, you will have to know what you want to buy. As an example, I decided to look for a 1 x 1 black brick to buy. From Bricklink's home page, you have a few options to find a part. The fastest way is to use catalog tab on the home page.

You can also search, which is just as fast—key in "1 x 1 black brick" in the search.

NOTE: sure you When keying size 2 x 2", as use spaces, such The search function is pretty opposed to "2n, persnickety.

Clicking the catalog tab will open reference catalog. How you'll begin to get an idea big the LEGO element library is. Since you are looking for a LEGO part, you can click on the Parts link.

If you want to browse, this is a good place to start, as the categories are broad enough to easily poke through.

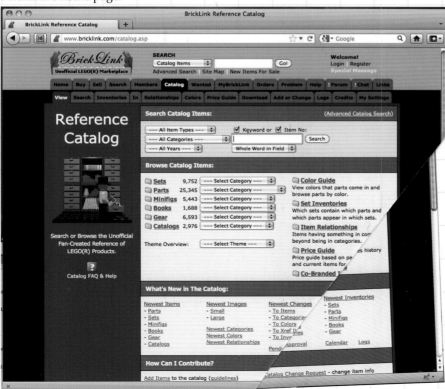

Bricklink's home page.

Bricklink's reference catalog.

The parts catalog is, in a word, *big*. At this point, unless you're browsing, you really need to know what you are looking for. Since we do, we can click on the "Brick" link. You can see the diversity of parts, even with brick (arches, modified bricks, etc.). This sometimes makes it hard to find a part, but I'll show you how I look for a part in a couple of pages.

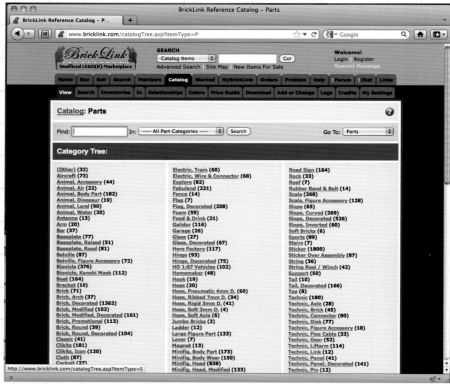

Bricklink's parts index

Boon.

That's g found the bricks! path, seen— now look at your *Catalog: Par*er the tabs: to know, as you'k. This is good backtrack, or woy need to lose your place if you may search box.   e the

We wanted a 1 x 1 black b click on the part number on so left. **The part number is a reference number that is listed on a. the parts in this book. With that, you can search Bricklink by going to the search box, keying in the part number, and searching "Parts"!**

Zeroing in on the 1 x 1 rick

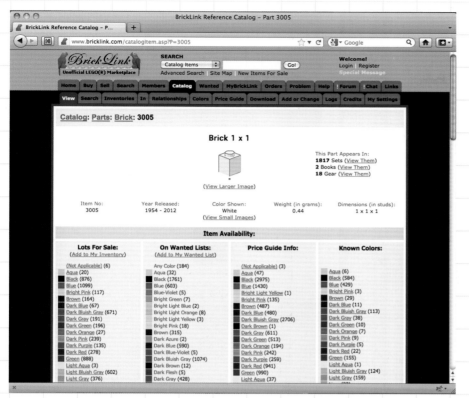

1 x 1 brick listings

When you click on the number, you'll get the part listing. What's important to you is the column on the right: Known Colors. That's a listing of colors that the 1 x 1 brick has been made in. Click on "Black" — the number in parentheses is the number of lots that are on sale with black 1 x 1 bricks, so we are almost at our destination!

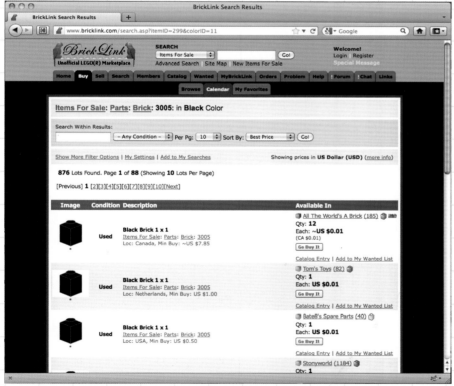

1 x 1 black brick vendor listings

And here are all the listings for black 1 x 1 bricks. You can sort by price and quantity, among other things.

The listings include the shop, its location, the price and the amount of parts available. It's a good idea when ordering different parts to try to minimize the number of vendors you're buying from to save on shipping costs. You can see what else a vendor is selling by clinking on their ink in the listing.

Identifying Parts

Shopping for a part is easy if you know what the part is. If you haven't gotten the slightest idea what the part is, you're going to have to figure out how to do this.

I use Peeron (www.peeron.com) when I am looking for a part name. Peeron is a parts inventory site for LEGO elements and has been around for some time. As a result, it has some pretty extensive parts libraries.

If you have the part on hand to buy, it's very easy to figure out what it is—most parts have a number on them to identify. Also, LEGO instructions also have part inventories with reference numbers for parts. As I mentioned before, the parts in this book all have their numbers listed.

However, there are older parts that don't have a reference. When I don't have a reference, I go to Peeron. I usually have an idea of what that part is, like "that odd landing gear piece."

That's not going to go very far in searching, so the first thing you need to know is the size of the part—it's footprint, so to speak.

In this example, I am looking for a 1 x 1 brick, so I am starting by using the part's footprint, 1 x 1, in the search box. Again, spaces are important. I also specify parts on the search.

The result is a list of parts that fit the 1 x 1 footprint. That's not too useful, but the link to show pictures is!

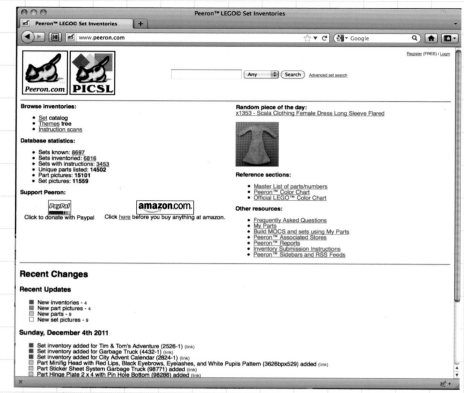

Peeron's homepage

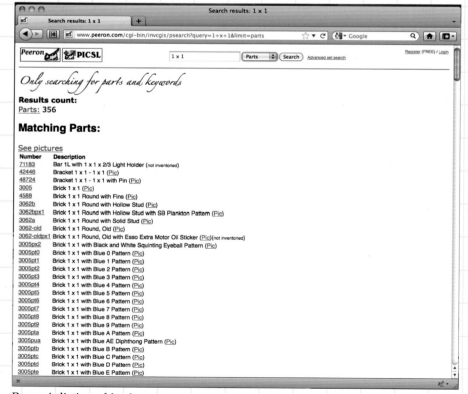

Peeron's listing of 1 x 1 parts

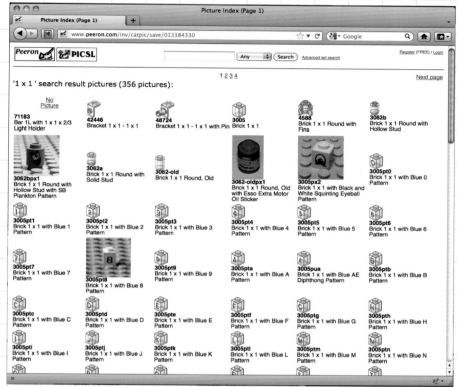

Peeron's visual index of 1 x 1 elements

Searching is much easier when you can see what you are looking for! Now you go through the pages of pics to find your part.

Bricklink can search, but not in this manner. However, Bricklink has a more recent listing of parts. For me, though, this is perfect for most of my searches.

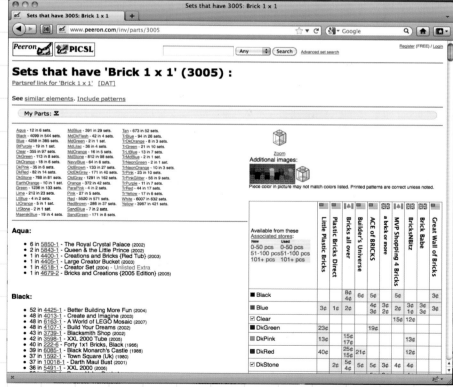

The 1 x 1 brick index on Peeron

When the 1 x 1 brick is clicked, you go to its page, and like Bricklink, it has a listing of colors. However, it also has a set listing for each color, so you can check to see if one of your sets has the part. There's also a listing of vendors who sell the part on Bricklink, as well as the part price. At this point, I usually copy the part number and look on Bricklink, as there are a lot of vendors to check on, near and far.

Miniland Figure

One of the trademark attractions at the LEGO-Land parks is the Miniland LEGO displays. Designed and built by the LEGO Master Builders at each park, these layouts are in a larger scale than minifigure scale, to allow more detailed buildings and vehicles to be built.

Didier Enjary, a LEGO fan in France, ran a series of articles in *BrickJournal* magazine about miniland figures, and will be returning soon with a new series on the scale.

A Miniland character uses bricks and a couple of Technic parts to build anything that is needed on the character. This is a simple, generic figure. You can change the figure in any number of ways, from building bent arms to adding color. (He can be wearing a striped shirt and jeans!)

With a few more basic parts, his pose can also be changed. Or his hairdo. See what you can do with the parts you have on hand!

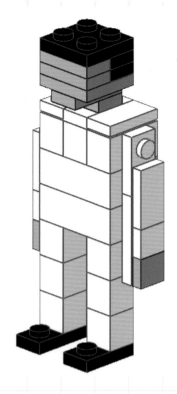

Qty	Part	Description	Color
2	30039.dat	Tile 1 x 1 with Groove	White
2	3623.dat	Plate 1 x 3	White
2	3700.dat	Technic Brick 1 x 2 with Hole	White
1	3004.dat	Brick 1 x 2	White
2	3023.dat	Plate 1 x 2	White
2	3002.dat	Brick 2 x 3	White
4	3069b.dat	Tile 1 x 2 with Groove	White
1	3794.dat	Plate 1 x 2 with 1 Stud	White
6	3005.dat	Brick 1 x 1	White
2	30039.dat	Tile 1 x 1 with Groove	Tan
1	3022.dat	Plate 2 x 2	Tan
2	3023.dat	Plate 1 x 2	Tan
1	3794.dat	Plate 1 x 2 with 1 Stud	Tan
1	3024.dat	Plate 1 x 1	Tan
1	3022.dat	Plate 2 x 2	Black
4	3023.dat	Plate 1 x 2	Black
2	4274.dat	Technic Pin 1/2	Blue

1 1x

2 1x

3 1x

4 1x

5 1x

6 1x

7 1x

8 1x 2x

9 2x

10 2x

11 2x

12 2x

13

1 1x

2 1x

3 1x

4 1x 1x

5 1x 1x

6 1x

14

1 1x 1x

2 1x

3 1x

4 1x

2x

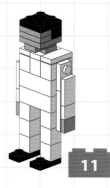

Sculpture

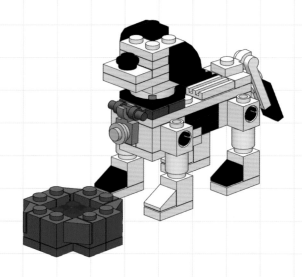

Lucky

This model set was done for a project that never got underway. I was asked to make models using LEGO Digital Designer (free design software you can download at *http://ldd.lego.com/*) that would be low in part count and 'cute.' The first thing that crossed my mind was to build a dog I quickly named Lucky.

I wanted some playability to the dog, so instead of being a static model, I articulated his legs, tail and head. As a result, he can sit and lay down as well as turn his head.

The other detail that I added was making one ear taller than the other, so Lucky looks like he is listening to something. He can also be built with different colors, so don't feel like he has to always be black and white!

Now, he needs a home and a couple of dog toys—can you build them?

Qty	Part	Description	Color
1	3024.dat	Plate 1 x 1	White
1	4032a.dat	Plate 2 x 2 Round with Axlehole Type 1	White
4	3700.dat	Technic Brick 1 x 2 with Hole	White
2	3794.dat	Plate 1 x 2 with 1 Stud	White
4	3062b.dat	Brick 1 x 1 Round with Hollow Stud	White
1	3795.dat	Plate 2 x 6	White
1	2412b.dat	Tile 1 x 2 Grille with Groove	White
1	2420.dat	Plate 2 x 2 Corner	White
1	6019.dat	Plate 1 x 1 with Clip Horizontal	White
2	3021.dat	Plate 2 x 3	White
2	50746.dat	Slope Brick 31 1 x 1 x 2/3	White
4	6541.dat	Technic Brick 1 x 1 with Hole	White
2	3022.dat	Plate 2 x 2	White
6	3023.dat	Plate 1 x 2	White
4	3005.dat	Brick 1 x 1	White
4	4070.dat	Brick 1 x 1 with Headlight	Red
1	2540.dat	Plate 1 x 2 with Handle	Red

Qty	Part	Description	Color
4	2420.dat	Plate 2 x 2 Corner	Red
4	50746.dat	Slope Brick 31 1 x 1 x 2/3	Red
1	3022.dat	Plate 2 x 2	Red
1	3023.dat	Plate 1 x 2	Red
4	3005.dat	Brick 1 x 1	Red
1	4073.dat	Plate 1 x 1 Round	Yellow
1	3024.dat	Plate 1 x 1	Black
2	6091.dat	Brick 2 x 1 x 1 & 1/3 with Curved Top	Black
4	2780.dat	Technic Pin with Friction and Slots	Black
1	3680.dat	Turntable 2 x 2 Plate Base	Black
1	2412b.dat	Tile 1 x 2 Grille with Groove	Black
2	50746.dat	Slope Brick 31 1 x 1 x 2/3	Black
1	4073.dat	Plate 1 x 1 Round	Black
2	3022.dat	Plate 2 x 2	Black
1	3023.dat	Plate 1 x 2	Black
1	3679.dat	~Turntable 2 x 2 Plate Top	Light Bluish Gray
1	6019.dat	Plate 1 x 1 with Clip Horizontal	Light Bluish Gray
4	3024.dat	Plate 1 x 1	Trans Dark Blue

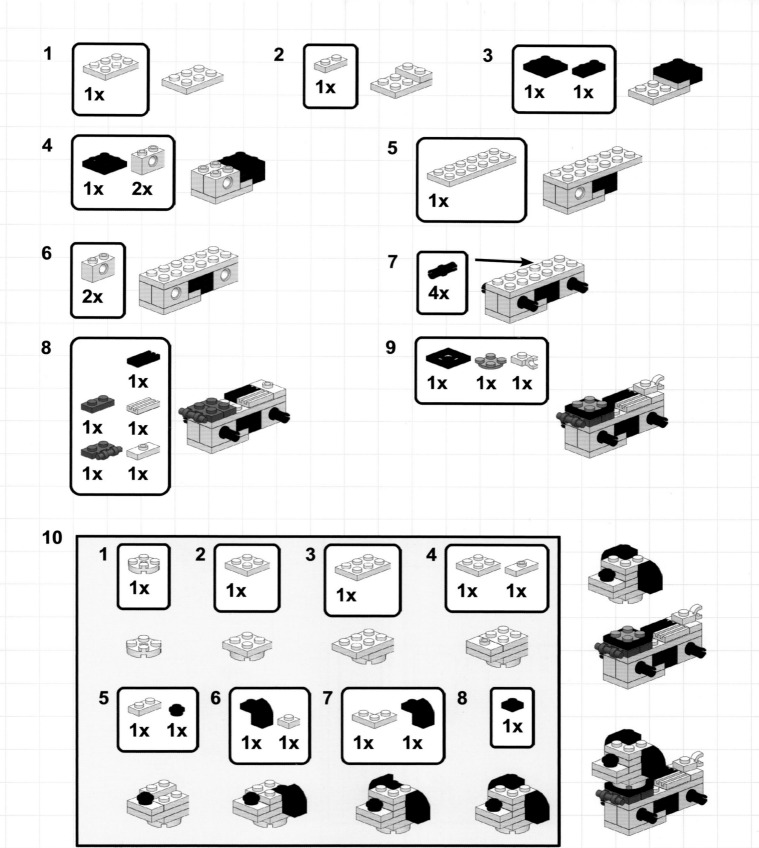

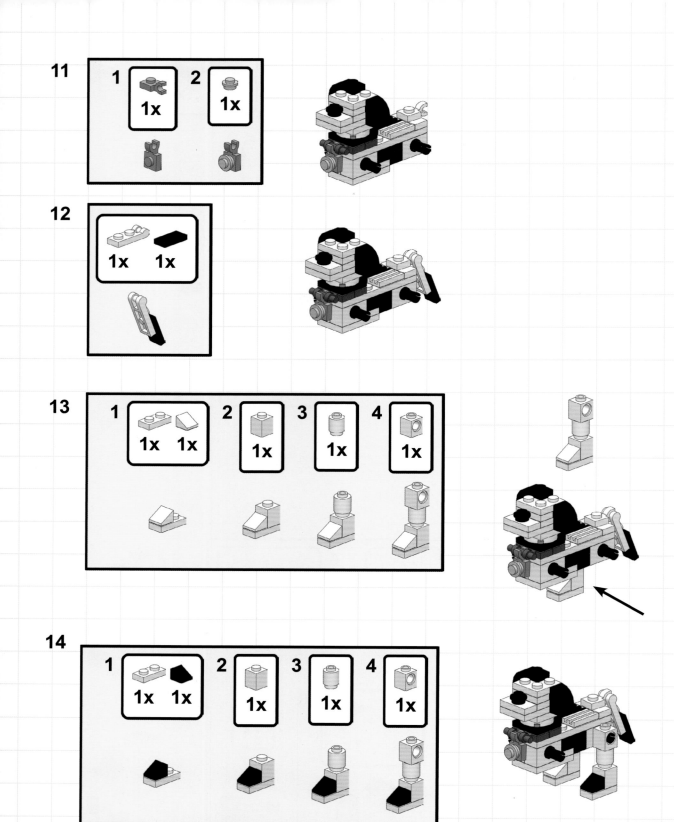

11

1 1x 2 1x

12 1x 1x

13 1 1x 1x 2 1x 3 1x 4 1x

14 1 1x 1x 2 1x 3 1x 4 1x

14

Sculpture

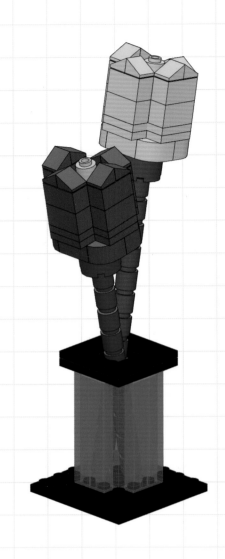

Tulips

This was the commemorative kit for the 2011 BrickMagic LEGO Festival in Raleigh, North Carolina (for more information on this annual event, go to *www.brickmagic.org*). Event kits are custom designed sets that are sold exclusively at fan events. Designing this set, I had to make a design that was relatively easy to build, used around 100 parts, and was something that was unique. Because BrickMagic fell on Mother's Day, it was decided to make a flower-based design. This is also something girls would enjoy building as well as boys.

The original design was done with a white vase, as the tall elements are easily found. This was quickly changed when the more rare transparent bricks became available. The vase can be filled after the flowers are inserted with 1 x 1 round plates to add some "soil" inside.

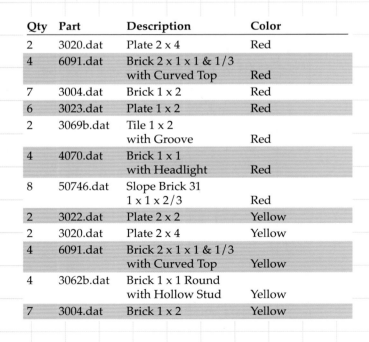

Qty	Part	Description	Color
2	3020.dat	Plate 2 x 4	Red
4	6091.dat	Brick 2 x 1 x 1 & 1/3 with Curved Top	Red
7	3004.dat	Brick 1 x 2	Red
6	3023.dat	Plate 1 x 2	Red
2	3069b.dat	Tile 1 x 2 with Groove	Red
4	4070.dat	Brick 1 x 1 with Headlight	Red
8	50746.dat	Slope Brick 31 1 x 1 x 2/3	Red
2	3022.dat	Plate 2 x 2	Yellow
2	3020.dat	Plate 2 x 4	Yellow
4	6091.dat	Brick 2 x 1 x 1 & 1/3 with Curved Top	Yellow
4	3062b.dat	Brick 1 x 1 Round with Hollow Stud	Yellow
7	3004.dat	Brick 1 x 2	Yellow

Qty	Part	Description	Color
6	3023.dat	Plate 1 x 2	Yellow
2	3069b.dat	Tile 1 x 2 with Groove	Yellow
4	4070.dat	Brick 1 x 1 with Headlight	Yellow
8	50746.dat	Slope Brick 31 1 x 1 x 2/3	Yellow
23	3062b.dat	Brick 1 x 1 Round with Hollow Stud	Green
2	3941.dat	Brick 2 x 2 Round	Green
4	2454.dat	Brick 1 x 2 x 5	Trans Med Blue
1	3031.dat	Plate 4 x 4	Black
6	3023.dat	Plate 1 x 2	Black
1	3958.dat	Plate 6 x 6	Black
2	2431.dat	Tile 1 x 4 with Groove	Black
2	3069b.dat	Tile 1 x 2 with Groove	Black

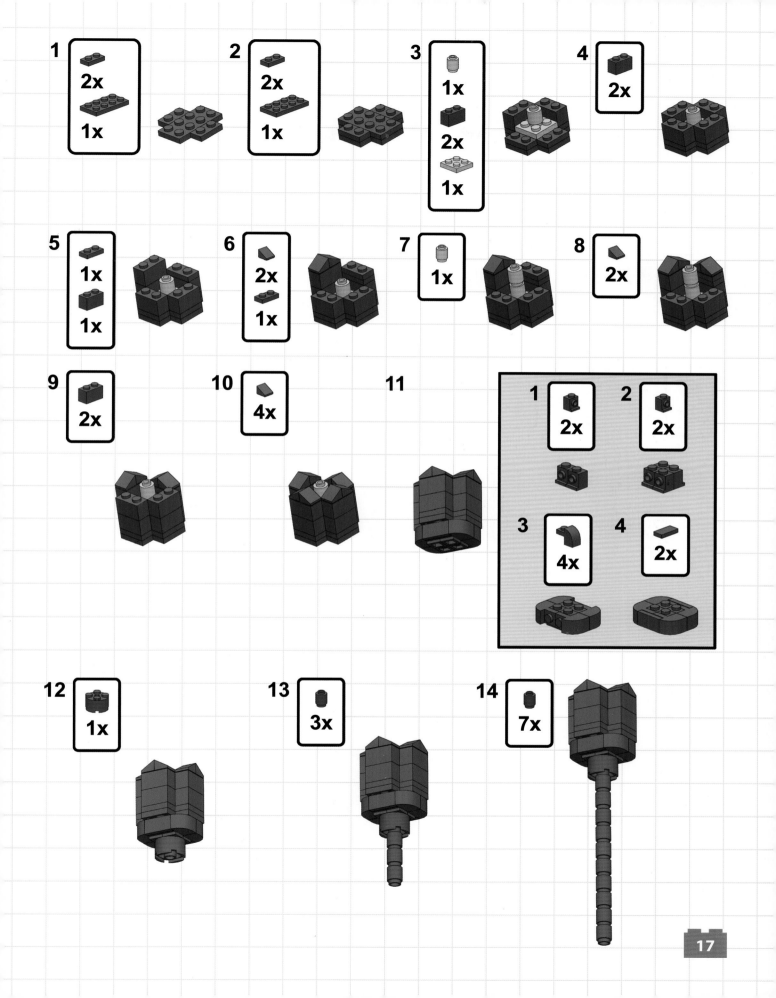

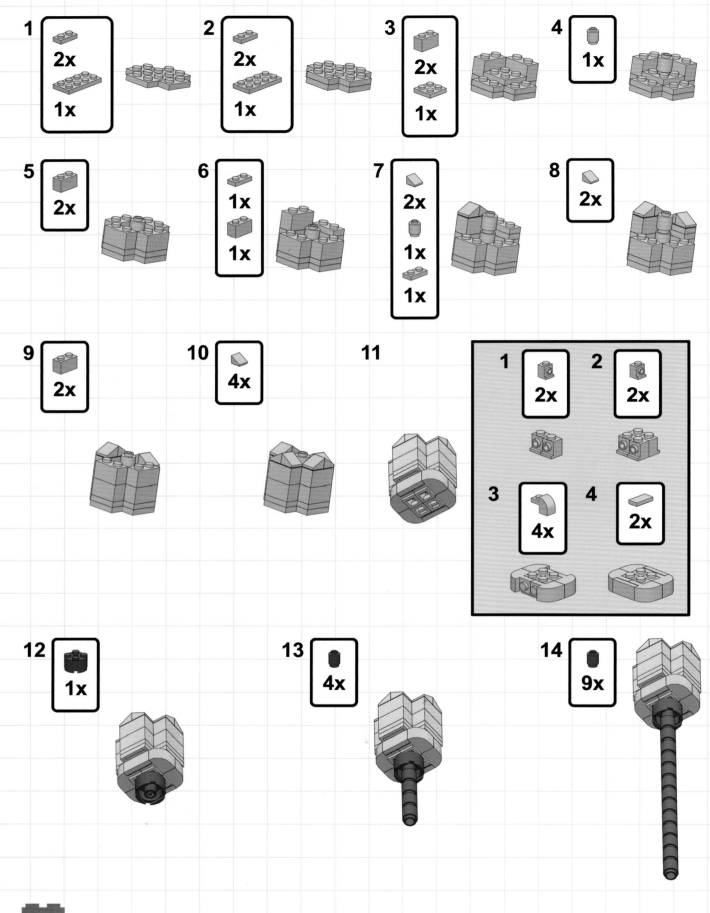

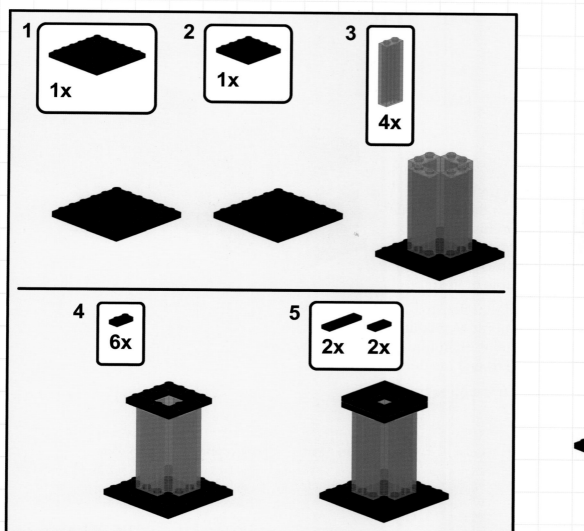

1 1x

2 1x

3 4x

4 6x

5 2x 2x

Order the complete BrickMagic Tulip Kit: only $12 plus shipping (includes 111 parts)

This Limited Edition set was custom designed by *BrickJournal* editor Joe Meno for the 2011 *BrickMagic LEGO Festival* in Raleigh, North Carolina, and contains 111 LEGO pieces. While supplies last, you can order the complete kit at this link:

http://twomorrows.com/index.php?main_page=product_info&products_id=902

NOTE: CHOKING HAZARD! Contains small parts. Not intended for children under 3. This is not a LEGO® Product. These are re-used LEGO elements that have been repackaged or altered from their original form. LEGO is a trademark of the LEGO Group, which does not sponsor, authorize or endorse this product. The LEGO Group is not liable for any loss, injury or damage arising from the use or misuse of this product.

Fire Engine

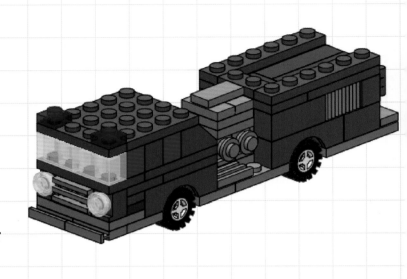

This model is from one of the first issues of *BrickJournal*, and built by Allan Bedford. You might have heard of him from his book, *The Unofficial Guide to LEGO Building*. He also wrote some articles and was the Copy Editor on *BrickJournal* in its first couple of years.

His fire engine is a nice build that doesn't use very much beyond commonly available bricks. The scale is a little smaller than mini-figure, as there is no space to fit one inside.

See if you can build another fire engine from this design!

Qty	Part	Description	Color
2	3004.dat	Brick 1 x 2	Trans Clear
2	6141.dat	Plate 1 x 1 Round	Trans Clear
4	4624.dat	Wheel Center Small	White
2	3622.dat	Brick 1 x 3	Red
2	3666.dat	Plate 1 x 6	Red
2	3623.dat	Plate 1 x 3	Red
2	2921.dat	Brick 1 x 1 with Handle	Red
1	3031.dat	Plate 4 x 4	Red
2	4070.dat	Brick 1 x 1 with Headlight	Red
4	3794.dat	Plate 1 x 2 with 1 Stud	Red
1	3795.dat	Plate 2 x 6	Red
2	3020.dat	Plate 2 x 4	Red
2	2420.dat	Plate 2 x 2 Corner	Red
2	3040b.dat	Slope Brick 45 2 x 1	Red
1	3022.dat	Plate 2 x 2	Red
6	3710.dat	Plate 1 x 4	Red
2	3004.dat	Brick 1 x 2	Red
4	3659.dat	Arch 1 x 4	Red
2	3023.dat	Plate 1 x 2	Red
2	3005.dat	Brick 1 x 1	Red
2	3024.dat	Plate 1 x 1	Dark Bluish Gray
2	2431.dat	Tile 1 x 4 with Groove	Dark Bluish Gray

Qty	Part	Description	Color
1	3069b.dat	Tile 1 x 2 with Groove	Dark Bluish Gray
4	30244.dat	Tile 1 x 2 Grille with Groove	Light Bluish Gray
2	32028.dat	Plate 1 x 2 with Door Rail	Light Bluish Gray
1	3031.dat	Plate 4 x 4	Light Bluish Gray
1	2431.dat	Tile 1 x 4 with Groove	Light Bluish Gray
6	4070.dat	Brick 1 x 1 with Headlight	Light Bluish Gray
4	3794.dat	Plate 1 x 2 with 1 Stud	Light Bluish Gray
1	3795.dat	Plate 2 x 6	Light Bluish Gray
3	2877.dat	Brick 1 x 2 with Grille	Light Bluish Gray
6	3020.dat	Plate 2 x 4	Light Bluish Gray
1	3002.dat	Brick 2 x 3	Light Bluish Gray
3	3021.dat	Plate 2 x 3	Light Bluish Gray
1	3022.dat	Plate 2 x 2	Light Bluish Gray
2	3069b.dat	Tile 1 x 2 with Groove	Light Bluish Gray
1	3023.dat	Plate 1 x 2	Light Bluish Gray
4	6141.dat	Plate 1 x 1 Round	Light Bluish Gray
4	3641.dat	Tyre 6/ 50 x 8 Offset Tread	Black
2	4600.dat	Plate 2 x 2 with Wheels Holder	Black
4	3004.dat	Brick 1 x 2	Blue
2	3024.dat	Plate 1 x 1	Trans Dark Blue

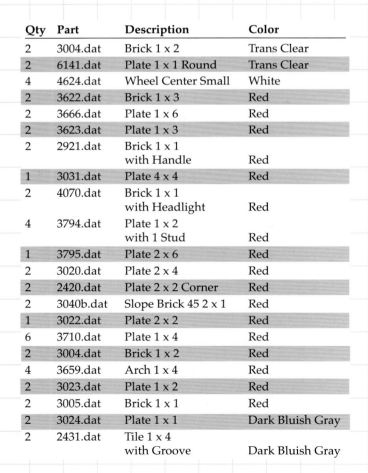

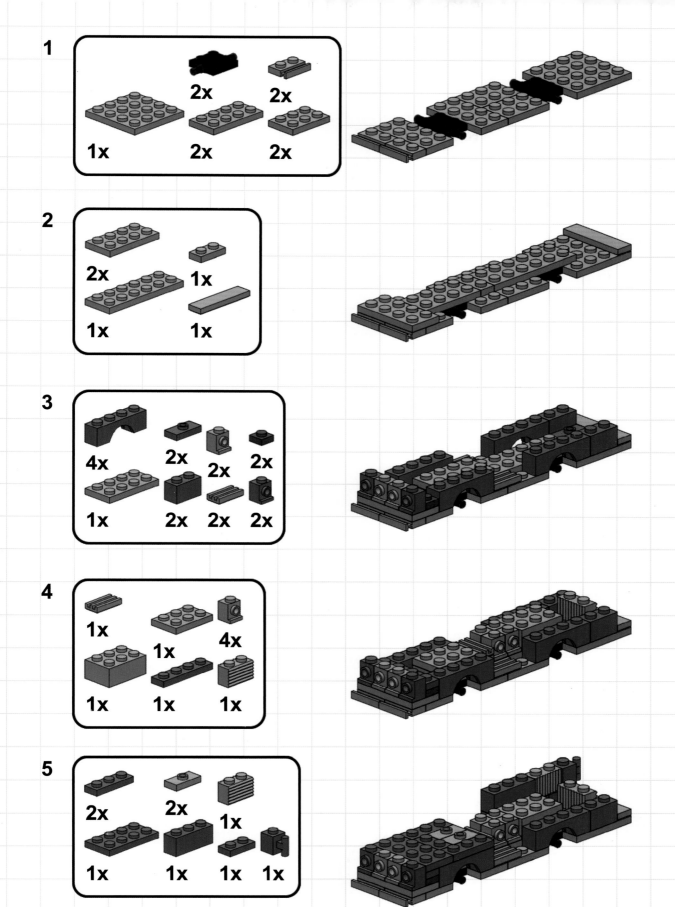

1

1x 2x 2x 2x 2x

2

2x 1x 1x 1x

3

4x 2x 2x 2x 1x 2x 2x 2x

4

1x 1x 4x 1x 1x 1x

5

2x 2x 1x 1x 1x 1x 1x

6

1x 1x 1x
1x 2x 2x

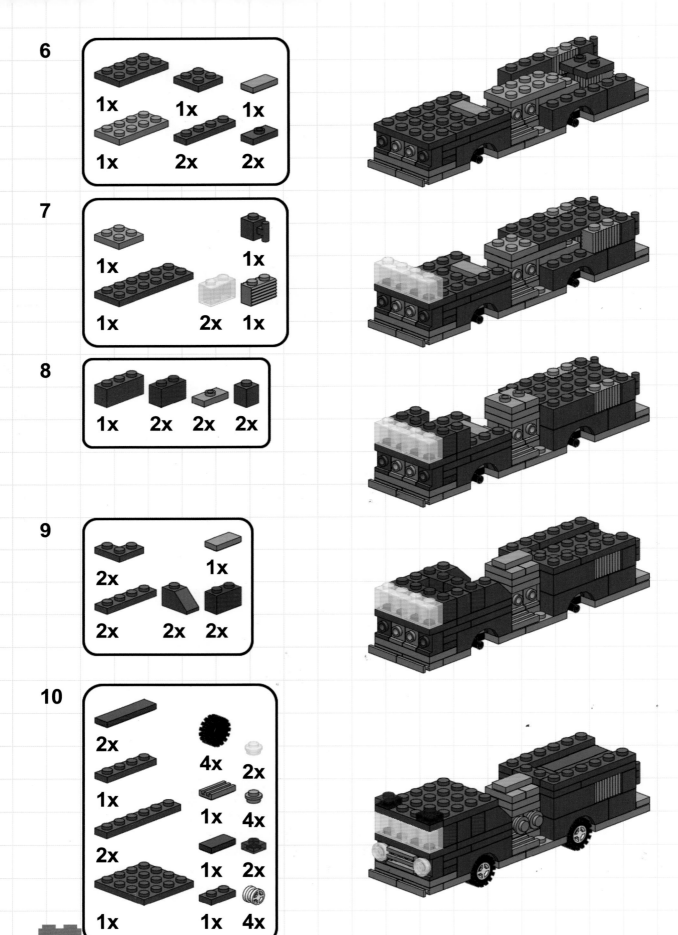

7

1x 1x
1x 2x 1x

8

1x 2x 2x 2x

9

2x 1x
2x 2x 2x

10

2x 4x 2x
1x 1x 4x
2x 1x 2x
1x 1x 4x

Streetside Vignette

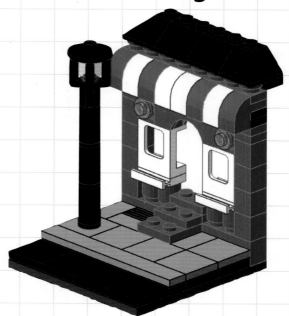

This is a creation by Geoff Gray, who is the Photo Editor for *BrickJournal*. This was first shown in the online edition of the magazine, to demonstrate how to build what is called a vignette in LEGO building.

A vignette is a "slice of life"—a small model of usually a figure or figures, and an environment to provide a context. This model is much like a movie set—it's open and only presents what is needed to make the setting clear. From here, figures can be added to make the scene come to life.

This can be extended to a longer stretch of sidewalk or more of the street, to fit in a car. It can also be extended vertically by adding more windows above the roofing.

What would you add to this vignette?

Qty	Part	Description	Color
2	32028.dat	Plate 1 x 2 with Door Rail	White
4	6091.dat	Brick 2 x 1 x 1 & 1/3 with Curved Top	White
2	2377.dat	Window 1 x 2 x 2 Plane	White
8	3005.dat	Brick 1 x 1	Red
2	3024.dat	Plate 1 x 1	Red
4	6091.dat	Brick 2 x 1 x 1 & 1/3 with Curved Top	Red
2	4070.dat	Brick 1 x 1 with Headlight	Red
4	3062b.dat	Brick 1 x 1 Round with Hollow Stud	Red
1	3008.dat	Brick 1 x 8	Red
2	3460.dat	Plate 1 x 8	Red
2	3022.dat	Plate 2 x 2	Red
8	4073.dat	Plate 1 x 1 Round	Red
1	3659.dat	Arch 1 x 4	Red
3	3023.dat	Plate 1 x 2	Red
1	3062b.dat	Brick 1 x 1 Round with Hollow Stud	Trans Yellow

Qty	Part	Description	Color
2	6141.dat	Plate 1 x 1 Round	Trans Yellow
1	2412b.dat	Tile 1 x 2 Grille with Groove	Dark Bluish Gray
1	41539.dat	Plate 8 x 8	Dark Bluish Gray
2	3673.dat	Technic Pin	Black
3	75535.dat	Technic Pin Joiner Round	Black
2	3039.dat	Slope Brick 45 2 x 2	Black
2	3045.dat	Slope Brick 45 2 x 2 Double Convex	Black
1	4740.dat	Dish 2 x 2 Inverted	Black
1	2566.dat	Plant Tree Palm Top	Black
2	3034.dat	Plate 2 x 8	Black
4	3460.dat	Plate 1 x 8	Black
4	3068b.dat	Tile 2 x 2 with Groove	Black
1	4162.dat	Tile 1 x 8	Light Bluish Gray
4	3068b.dat	Tile 2 x 2 with Groove	Light Bluish Gray
1	2460.dat	Tile 2 x 2 with Pin	Light Bluish Gray
3	3069b.dat	Tile 1 x 2 with Groove	Light Bluish Gray
1	4274.dat	Technic Pin 1/2	Blue

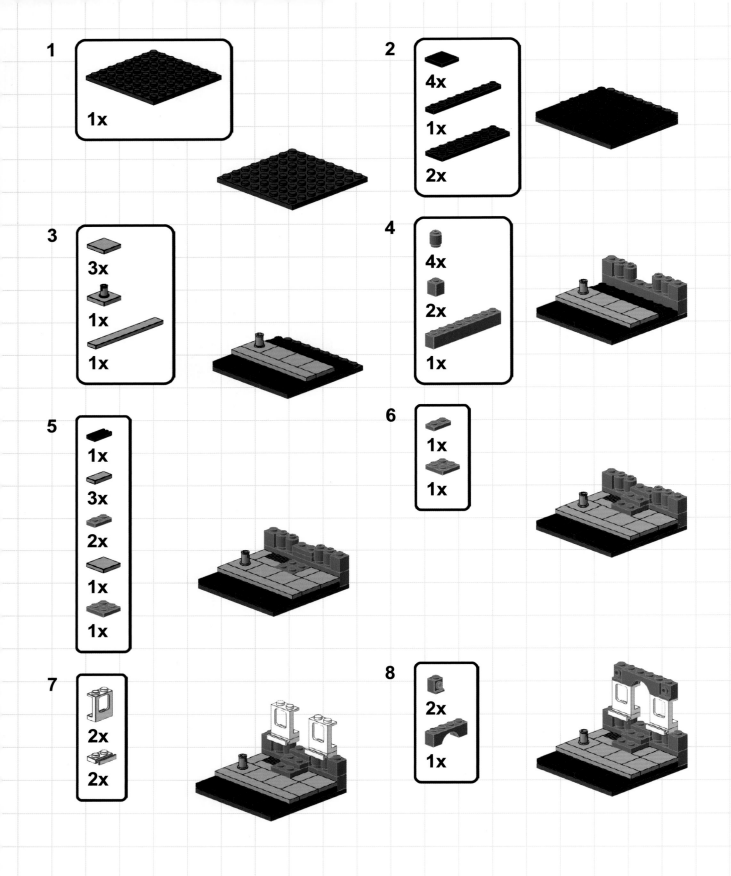

1 1x

2 4x 1x 2x

3 3x 1x 1x

4 4x 2x 1x

5 1x 3x 2x 1x 1x

6 1x 1x

7 2x 2x

8 2x 1x

9

6x

10

2x

11

2x

1x

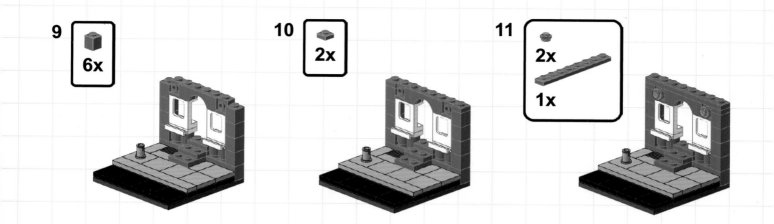

12

1

2x

2

4x 4x

3

1x

4

8x

5

2x

6

1x

7

2x

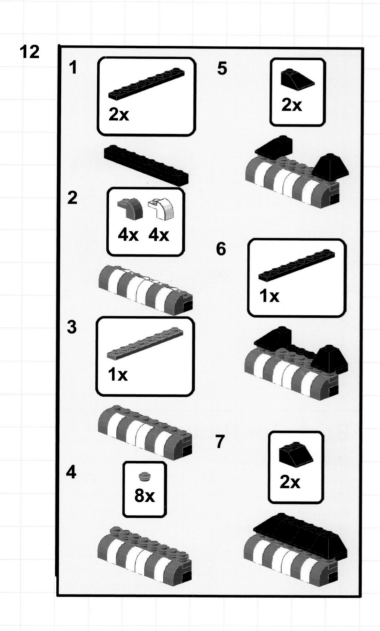

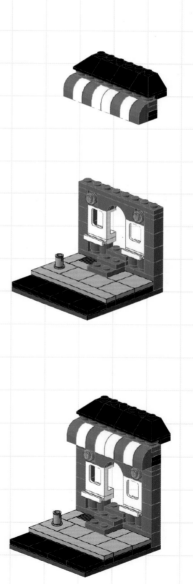

13

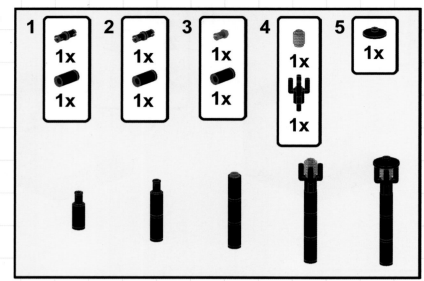

1	2	3	4	5
1x	1x	1x	1x	1x
1x	1x	1x	1x	
			1x	

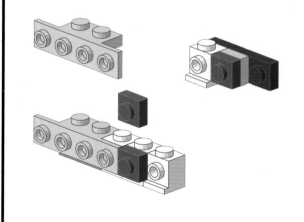

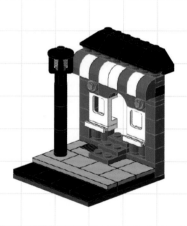

Bricks for Thought

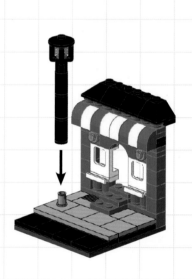

LEGO building can be challenging, especially when building studs sideways. A 1 x 1 headlight brick is a perfect solution, but has problems in building if you have to build a long section. Here are some solutions:

1 x 2 - 1 x 4 bracket placed beside the brick (note that the 1 x 2 plate on the bracket needs to be the same height as the brick). The bracket width fills in the space between a sideways plate and a brick edge. You can also go behind, as the thin side of the headlight brick is two plates thick.

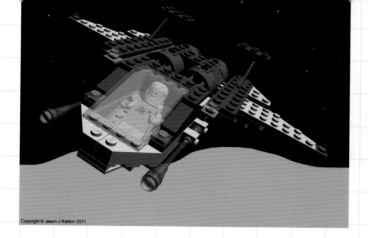

Copyright © Jason J Railton 2011

Drake Class VTOL/VG Ground Assault Fighter

by Jason Railton

The 'Drake' class is a Vertical Take-off and Landing (VTOL) / Variable Geometry (VG) fighter aircraft, originally designed for the air-to-ground combat role. Twin combination aerobic/anaerobic engines make it capable of operations from a land base, or orbital insertion from a carrier platform. Weapon variants further allow it to perform in air-to-air, bomber, or deep space fighter-escort roles.

The VTOL and heavy lift capability has also made it ideal for civilian use in law enforcement, fire fighting, medevac and even construction lifting in remote areas.

For take-off, landing, and hover manoeuvres the main engines turn vertical and the wings fold in to make the vehicle smaller. Additional stabilizing thrust is provided from a vent below the cockpit, ducted from the main engines. In forward flight, the engines transition to the horizontal position and the wings are deployed for stability at speed.

The docking spigot below the engines is used to lock the aircraft down to the landing platform in storm or surface-heave conditions, or where the landing platform itself is mobile or retractable. It is also used to dock to the side of orbital transports for interplanetary re-deployment. It provides refuelling and diagnostic connections.

Rumors of the two-seater 'Draco' variant are as yet neither officially confirmed nor denied.

Design Notes
I wanted to build a small space ship in the Classic Space style, and one that I could build multiples of for fitting to a larger carrier.

The swivelling engines come from the fighters in the introduction sequence of the video game *Raiden*. Modern VTOL fighter aircraft such as the Hawker Harrier and Yakovlev Yak-141 use ducted engine exhaust, or separate fans or engines for their vertical lift.

Only propeller aircraft such as the Bell-Boeing V-22 Osprey are able to rotate the engines (along with the propellers) for vertical thrust.

The fighters in *Raiden* look similar to swing-wing fighter aircraft, but the gearing would be more complex to make, say, an F-14 Tomcat style swing-wing, what with the engines having to pivot much further back in the aircraft body than the wings.

The gearing thus dictated the forward-sweeping wings, and the need to mount the gears underneath raised sides. The technicalities of achieving this came together quite quickly once those decisions were made.

The lowered pod-style cockpit is inspired by the fighters from *Space: Above and Beyond*, where the pilots get into cockpit modules in a small 'hangar' room before the CGI takes over to show the actual craft launching.

I also think the trans-yellow hinged cockpit was woefully under-used in Classic Space (I was deprived—I only ever had one!), and should have been used to keep the line going right up to the present day.

This model has previously appeared on display outside the LEGO Brand Store in Milton Keynes in England, at Legoworld in Zwolle in the Netherlands, and at various other Brickish Association events in the UK.

Construction Notes
The main difficulty is in correctly aligning the gears. Use the 14-tooth type of bevel gear from the original style of differential gear. Look closely at the diagram, and you'll see that turning one by 90° can change how they mesh. The modern 16-tooth type don't allow you to place meshing gears with their shafts rotated dead-on right-angles, and that's important here.

The wing mounts (the liftarms) should point straight out to the sides when both the engine block and the side strakes (the blue 2 x 8 plate bits) are held horizontal. As the engines are turned vertical, the wings should sag slightly and tuck in under the strakes in the forward position.

Qty	Part	Description	Color
1	3819.dat	Minifig Arm Left	White
1	3842b.dat	Minifig Helmet Classic with Thick Chin Guard	White
1	3815c01.dat	Minifig Hips and Legs (Complete)	White
1	3818.dat	Minifig Arm Right	White
1	3838.dat	Minifig Airtanks	White
1	973p90.dat	Minifig Torso with Classic Space Pattern	White
2	6141.dat	Plate 1 x 1 Round	Trans Red
2	3957.dat	Antenna 4H	Trans Red
2	4589.dat	Cone 1 x 1	Trans Red
2	3062b.dat	Brick 1 x 1 Round with Hollow Stud	Trans Red
4	3024.dat	Plate 1 x 1	Trans Red
1	4474.dat	Windscreen 6 x 4 x 2 Canopy	Trans Yellow
2	6141.dat	Plate 1 x 1 Round	Trans Yellow
4	3024.dat	Plate 1 x 1	Trans Yellow
3	4740.dat	Dish 2 x 2 Inverted	Trans Yellow
1	3626bp05.dat	Minifig Head with Standard Grin and Eyebrows Pattern	Yellow
2	3820.dat	Minifig Hand	Yellow
2	30039.dat	Tile 1 x 1 with Groove	Dark Bluish Gray
2	3941.dat	Brick 2 x 2 Round	Dark Bluish Gray
1	4032b.dat	Plate 2 x 2 Round with Axlehole Type 2	Dark Bluish Gray
2	30360.dat	Cylinder 3 x 6 x 2 2/3 Horizontal	Dark Bluish Gray
2	3023.dat	Plate 1 x 2	Dark Bluish Gray
2	32064a.dat	Technic Brick 1 x 2 with Axlehole Type 1	Green
1	3707.dat	Technic Axle 8	Black
2	4592c01.dat	Hinge Control Stick and Base (Complete)	Black
2	32062.dat	Technic Axle 2 Notched	Black
2	2825.dat	Technic Beam 4 x 0.5 Liftarm with Boss	Light Bluish Gray
4	2420.dat	Plate 2 x 2 Corner	Light Bluish Gray
2	3004.dat	Brick 1 x 2	Light Bluish Gray

Qty	Part	Description	Color
2	3020.dat	Plate 2 x 4	Light Bluish Gray
1	3022.dat	Plate 2 x 2	Light Bluish Gray
4	4143.dat	Technic Gear 14 Tooth Bevel	Light Bluish Gray
1	3710.dat	Plate 1 x 4	Light Bluish Gray
1	3934.dat	Wing 4 x 8 Right	Light Bluish Gray
1	3936.dat	Wing 4 x 4 Left	Light Bluish Gray
2	2412b.dat	Tile 1 x 2 Grille with Groove	Light Bluish Gray
4	4274.dat	Technic Pin 1/2	Light Bluish Gray
2	2462.dat	Brick 3 x 3 Facet	Light Bluish Gray
1	3010.dat	Brick 1 x 4	Light Bluish Gray
2	3956.dat	Bracket 2 x 2 - 2 x 2	Light Bluish Gray
8	4070.dat	Brick 1 x 1 with Headlight	Light Bluish Gray
2	4855.dat	Wedge 4 x 4 Triple Inverted	Light Bluish Gray
1	3673.dat	Technic Pin	Light Bluish Gray
1	3933.dat	Wing 4 x 8 Left	Light Bluish Gray
7	3023.dat	Plate 1 x 2	Light Bluish Gray
1	3039pc5.dat	Slope Brick 45 2 x 2 with Flight Control Pattern	Light Bluish Gray
4	2436.dat	Bracket 1 x 2 - 1 x 4	Light Bluish Gray
1	3795.dat	Plate 2 x 6	Light Bluish Gray
1	3935.dat	Wing 4 x 4 Right	Light Bluish Gray
2	3040b.dat	Slope Brick 45 2 x 1	Light Bluish Gray
2	4286.dat	Slope Brick 33 3 x 1	Blue
1	4315.dat	Hinge Plate 1 x 4 with Car Roof Holder	Blue
3	3710.dat	Plate 1 x 4	Blue
2	3479.dat	Tail 4 x 2 x 2	Blue
4	6541.dat	Technic Brick 1 x 1 with Hole	Blue
1	41770.dat	Wing 2 x 4 Left	Blue
1	41769.dat	Wing 2 x 4 Right	Blue
1	3010.dat	Brick 1 x 4	Blue
1	3003.dat	Brick 2 x 2	Blue
2	3039.dat	Slope Brick 45 2 x 2	Blue
4	3700.dat	Technic Brick 1 x 2 with Hole	Blue
2	3623.dat	Plate 1 x 3	Blue
2	3021.dat	Plate 2 x 3	Blue
3	3666.dat	Plate 1 x 6	Blue
2	3034.dat	Plate 2 x 8	Blue

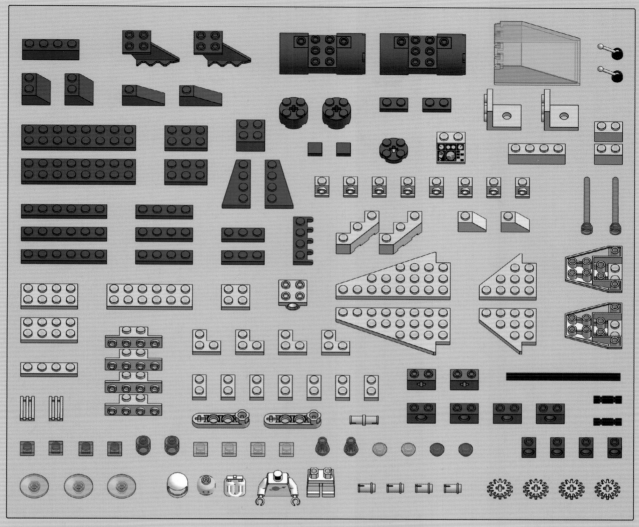

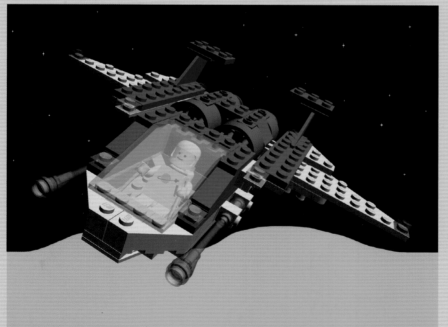

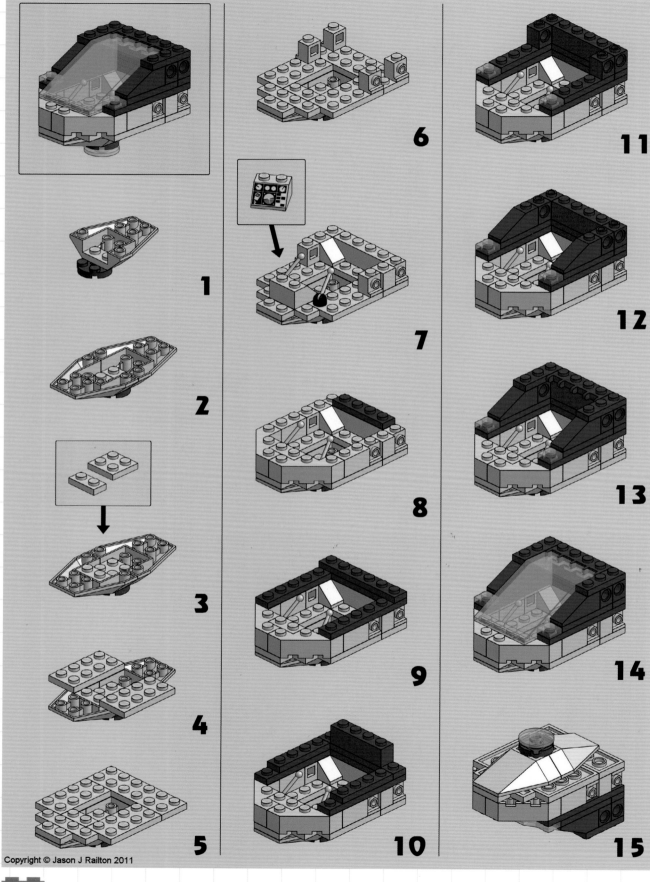

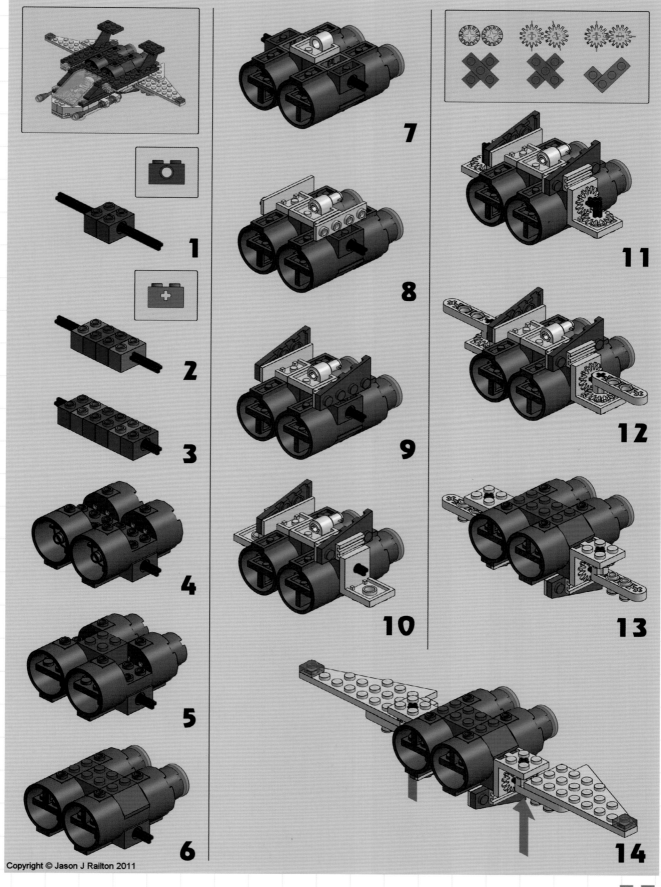

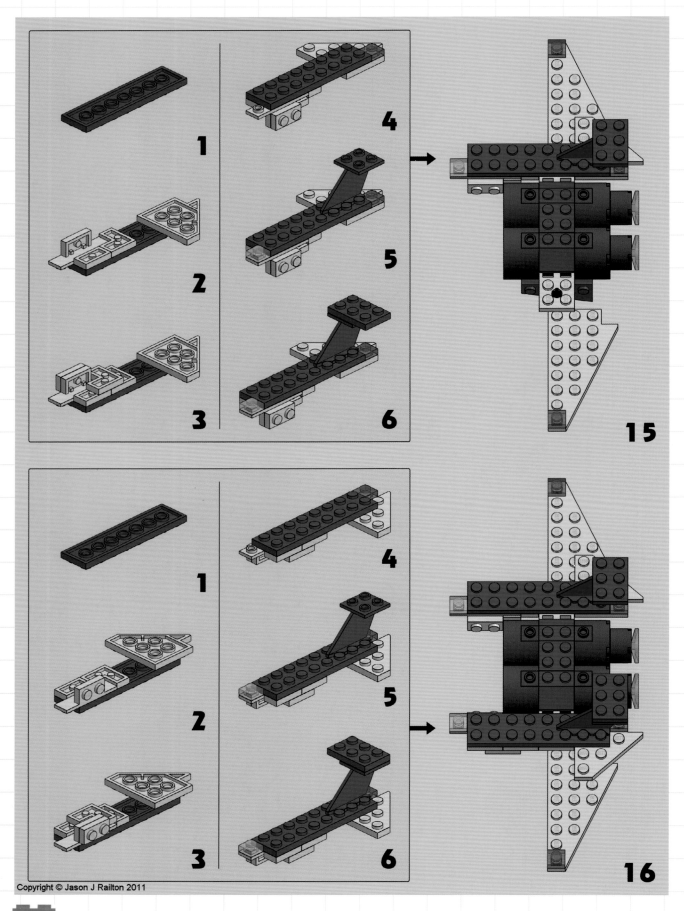

1

2

3

4

5

6

15

1

2

3

4

5

6

16

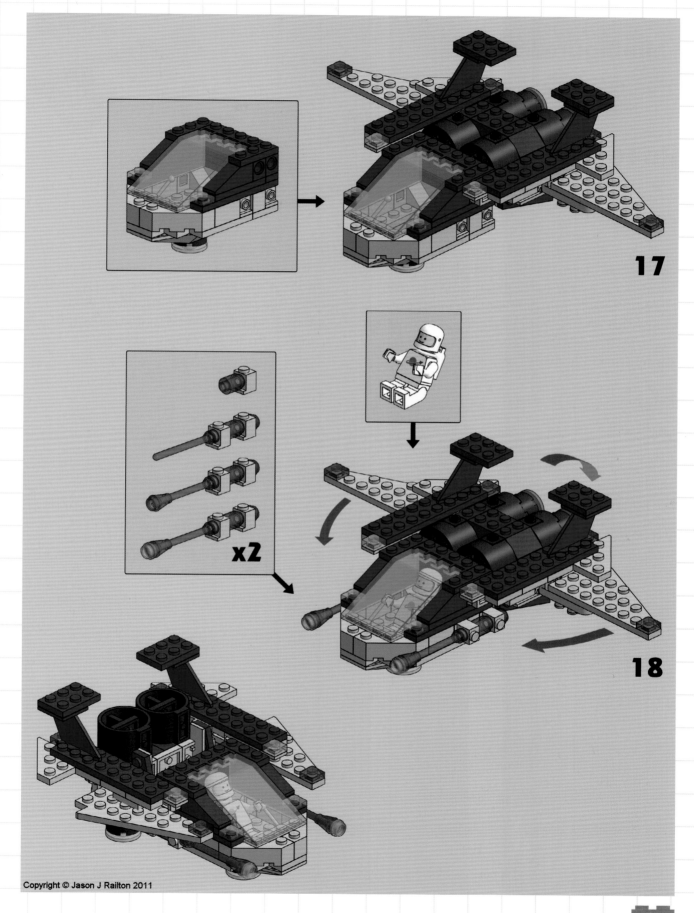

17

18

Minifigure Scale

Roadster

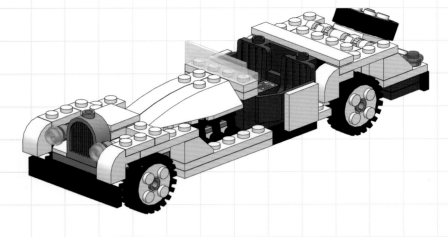

This is among the oldest models I have built. One of the first models I posted online, the Roadster was my early try at building something uniquely mine. The model is about ten years old, and in spite of a couple of updates in parts, it still remains on my shelf, and sometimes in layouts.

The main part that is needed in this model is the car base. This part recently came back into production at LEGO, so you may already have this part. I have built the roadster in red, green, and white. What color do you like, and can you build *your* roadster?

Qty	Part	Description	Color
1	30413.dat	Panel 1 x 4 x 1	Trans Clear
2	3022.dat	Plate 2 x 2	White
2	3005.dat	Brick 1 x 1	White
1	44568.dat	Hinge Plate 1 x 4 Locking with Two Single Fingers on Side	White
1	6636.dat	Tile 1 x 6	White
6	3040b.dat	Slope Brick 45 2 x 1	White
1	41747.dat	Wedge 2 x 6 Double Right	White
4	3023.dat	Plate 1 x 2	White
2	3623.dat	Plate 1 x 3	White
6	3710.dat	Plate 1 x 4	White
3	3666.dat	Plate 1 x 6	White
1	41748.dat	Wedge 2 x 6 Double Left	White
3	3068b.dat	Tile 2 x 2 with Groove	White
1	2460.dat	Tile 2 x 2 with Pin	White
2	6091.dat	Brick 2 x 1 x 1 & 1/3 with Curved Top	White
1	44570.dat	Hinge Car Roof 4 x 4 Locking	White
3	3795.dat	Plate 2 x 6	White
3	3010.dat	Brick 1 x 4	White
2	3832.dat	Plate 2 x 10	White
3	3020.dat	Plate 2 x 4	White
5	6248.dat	Wheel Basic with 4 Studs and Technic Peghole	White
2	4286.dat	Slope Brick 33 3 x 1	White

Qty	Part	Description	Color
2	6141.dat	Plate 1 x 1 Round	Trans Red
2	4073.dat	Plate 1 x 1 Round	Trans Yellow
2	3022.dat	Plate 2 x 2	Dark Bluish Gray
2	3069bpc1.dat	Tile 1 x 2 with Yellow Buttons and Knob Controls Pattern	Dark Bluish Gray
1	30149.dat	Car Base 4 x 5 with 2 Seats	Dark Bluish Gray
2	3710.dat	Plate 1 x 4	Dark Bluish Gray
2	3794.dat	Plate 1 x 2 with 1 Stud	Dark Bluish Gray
1	3020.dat	Plate 2 x 4	Dark Bluish Gray
5	3483.dat	Tyre Small	Black
2	6636.dat	Tile 1 x 6	Black
3	3023.dat	Plate 1 x 2	Black
4	3794.dat	Plate 1 x 2 with 1 Stud	Black
6	4599.dat	Tap 1 x 1	Black
2	2436.dat	Bracket 1 x 2 - 1 x 4	Black
2	3021.dat	Plate 2 x 3	Black
1	3031.dat	Plate 4 x 4	Light Bluish Gray
1	3710.dat	Plate 1 x 4	Light Bluish Gray
6	4070.dat	Brick 1 x 1 with Headlight	Light Bluish Gray
1	30147.dat	Car Grille 1 x 2 x 2 Round Top with Lights	Light Bluish Gray
2	30157.dat	Plate 2 x 4 with Pins	Light Bluish Gray

1

2x

3x

1x

2

2x

1x

3

2x

4

1x

3x

5

2x

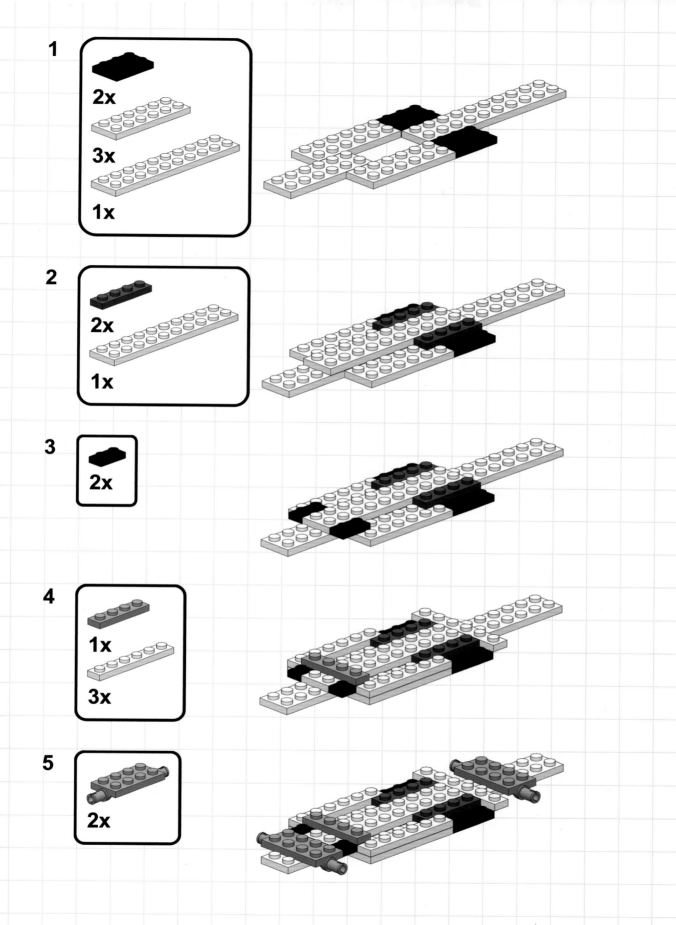

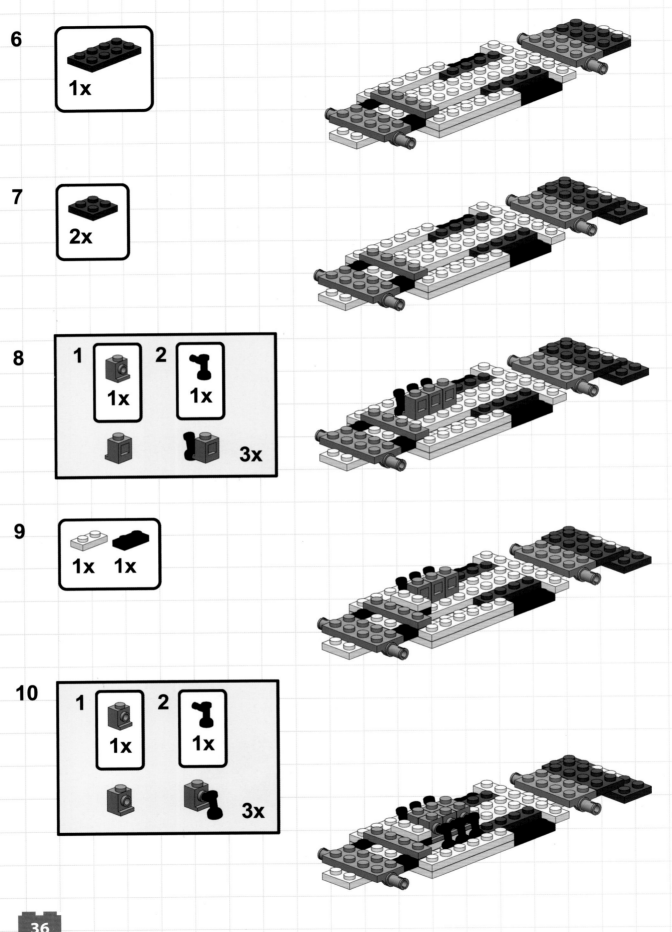

6   1x

7   2x

8   1   1x   2   1x   3x

9   1x   1x

10   1   1x   2   1x   3x

11 2x

12 2x

13 1x

14 2x

15 1x

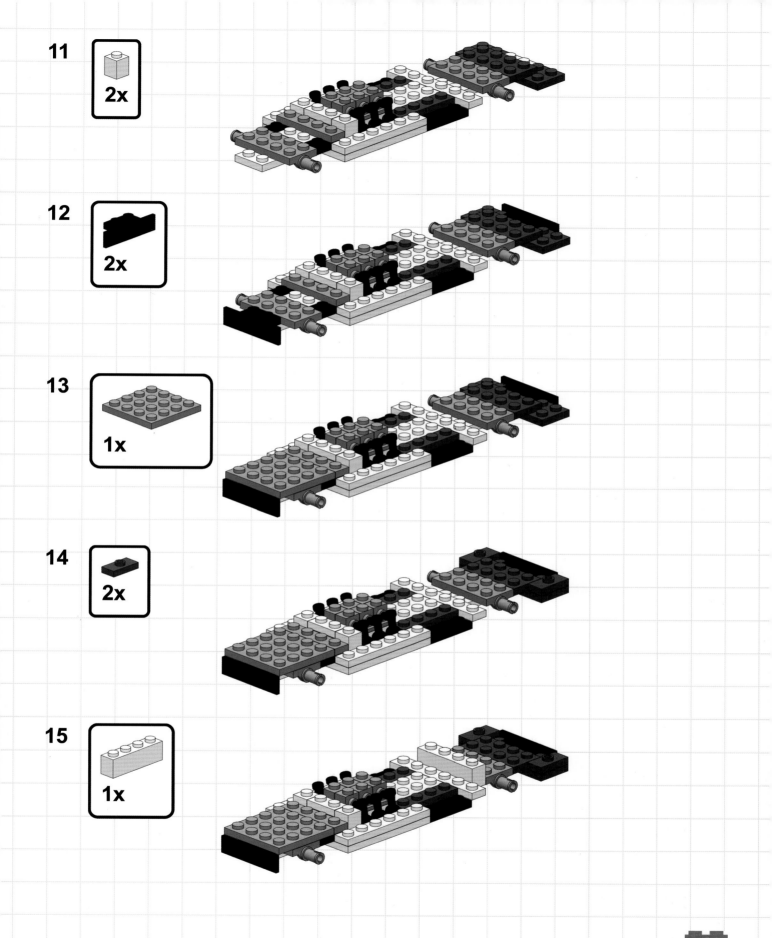

16

1x　2x

17

1x

18

2x

19

1x　1x　1x

20

1x

1x

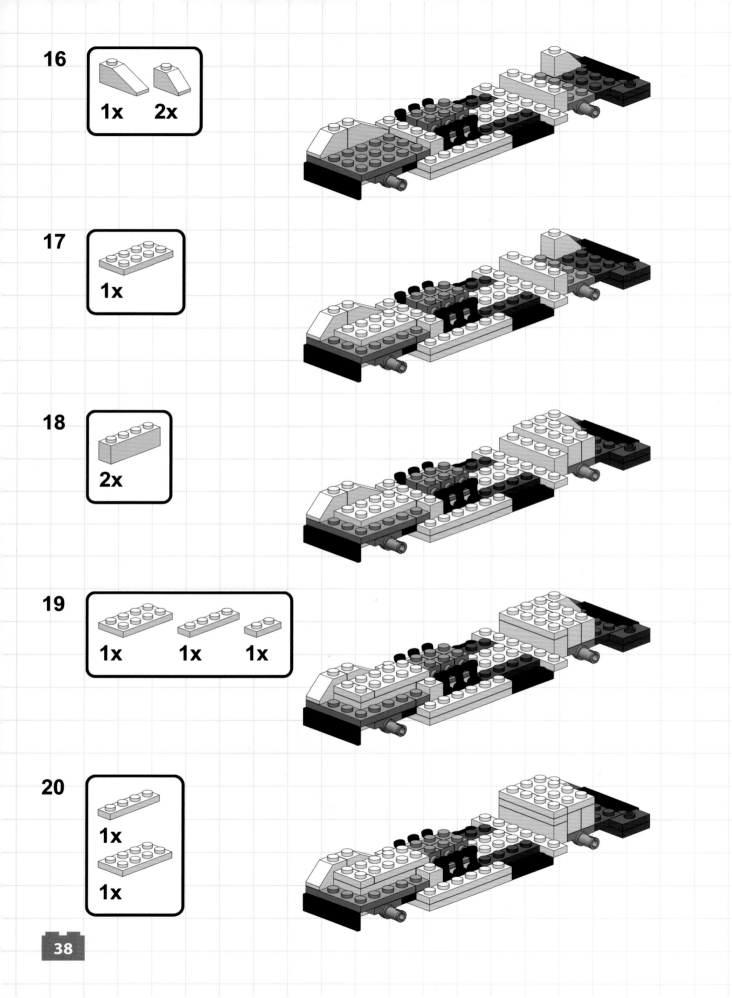

21

1x

22

1x 4x

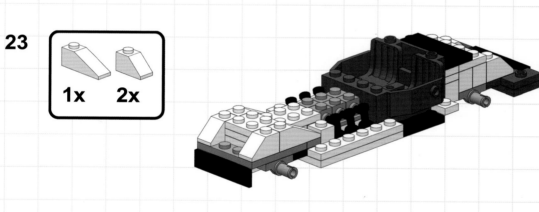

23

1x 2x

24

1x

1x

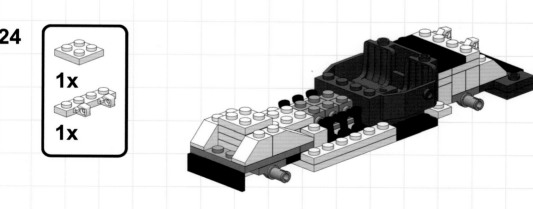

25

1 1x 1x

2 1x 1x

3 1x

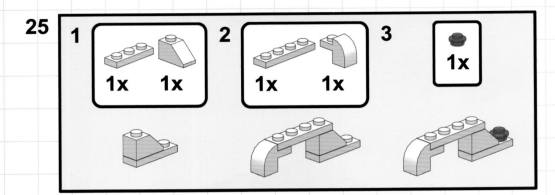

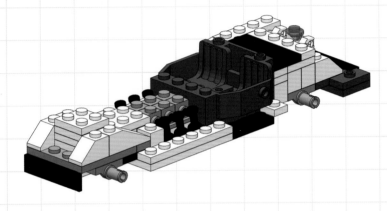

26

1 1x 1x

2 1x 1x

3 1x

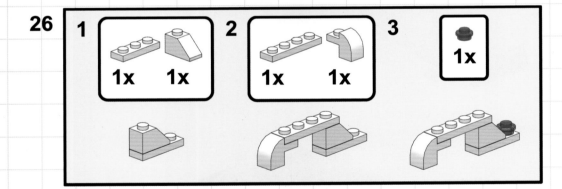

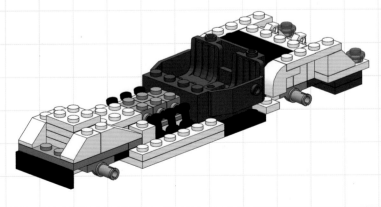

27

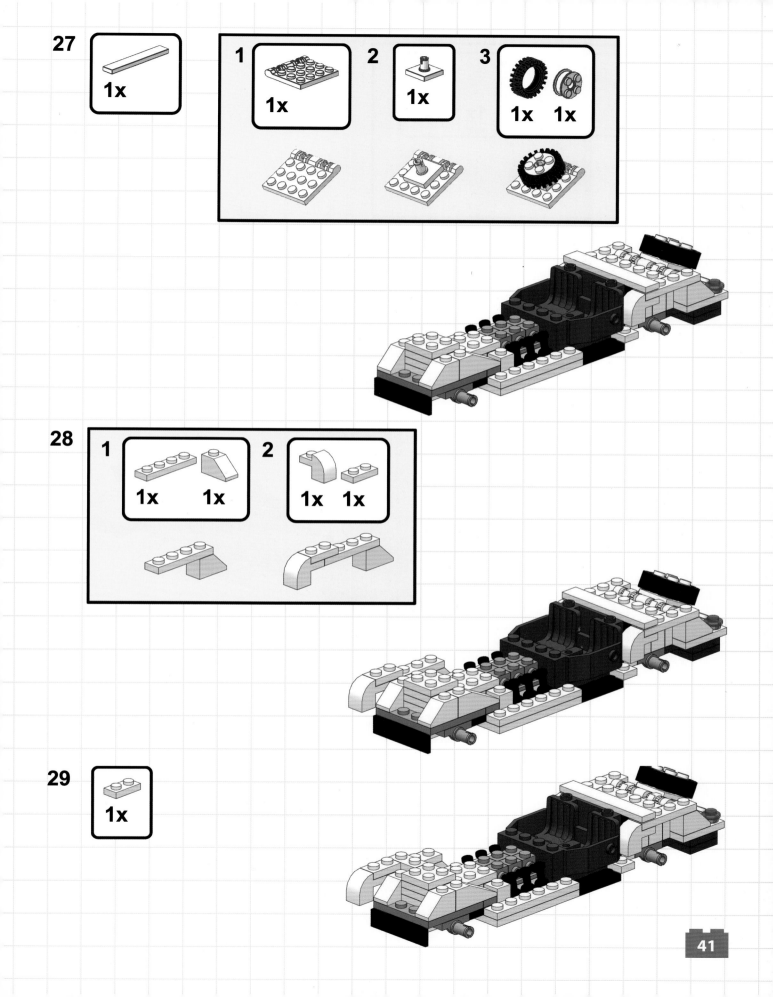

1x

1   1x   2   1x   3   1x   1x

28

1   1x   1x   2   1x   1x

29

1x

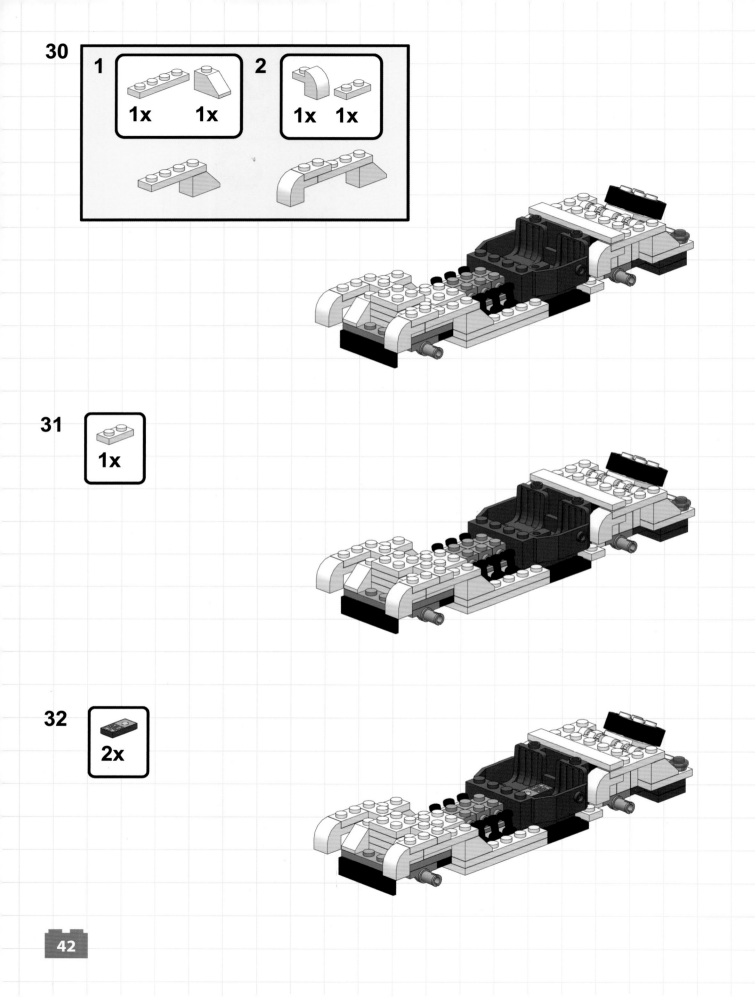

30

1 1x 1x

2 1x 1x

31 1x

32 2x

33

1x

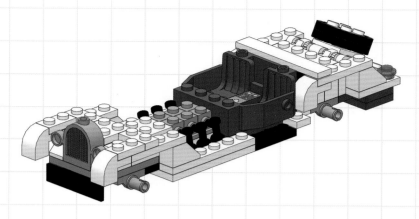

34

2x

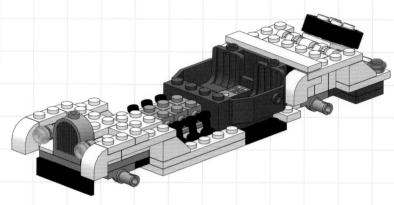

35

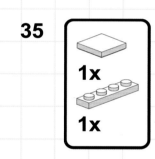

1x

1x

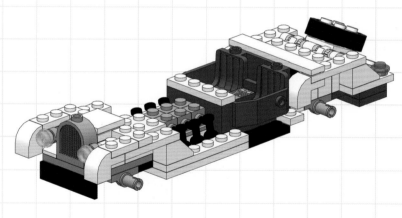

36

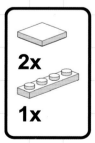

2x

1x

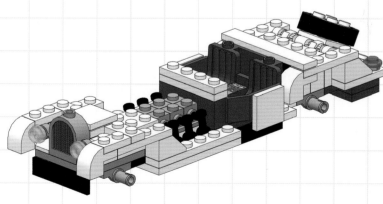

37

1x

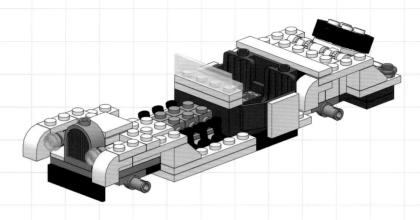

38

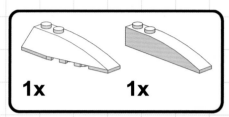

1x   **1x**

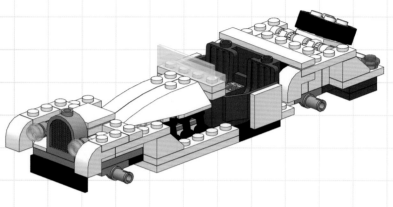

39

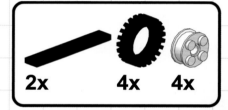

2x   **4x**   **4x**

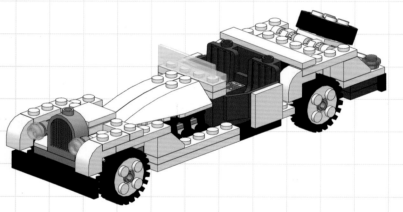

Bricks for Thought

How do you build SNOT-wise vertically? One way is to stack 2 plates between the SNOT (*Studs Not On Top*) elements. This allows a 1 stud gap to be made between the bricks, so a 1 x 3 plate can be fitted. From there, more plates and bricks can be added for more height. With elements held in place from vertical and horizontal planes, the result is a pretty strong construction.

Hot Rod

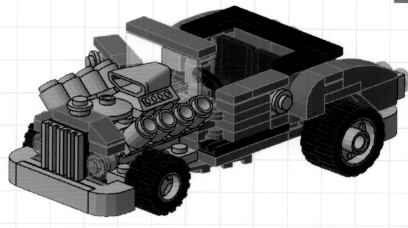

This hot rod was built for LEGO Factory about five years ago. Back then, I was working on a LEGO project creating a fan-designed set based on cool cars. At the time, I had a builder's block and could not build a car for a couple of weeks. I finally designed some after the deadline passed, so my designs showed up on the Cool Car Garage set as box art.

Parts List

Qty	Part	Description	Color
2	4864a.dat	Panel 1 x 2 x 2 with Solid Studs	Trans Clear
1	3069b.dat	Tile 1 x 2 with Groove	White
4	4073.dat	Plate 1 x 1 Round	Trans Red
4	3062b.dat	Brick 1 x 1 Round with Hollow Stud	Red
4	2429.dat	Hinge Plate 1 x 4 Base	Red
2	3022.dat	Plate 2 x 2	Red
1	2431.dat	Tile 1 x 4 with Groove	Red
2	87087.dat	Brick 1 x 1 with Stud on 1 Side	Red
2	3622.dat	Brick 1 x 3	Red
6	3023.dat	Plate 1 x 2	Red
2	50950.dat	Slope Brick Curved 3 x 1	Red
1	3032.dat	Plate 4 x 6	Red
2	3039.dat	Slope Brick 45 2 x 2	Red
1	3829a.dat	~Car Steering Wheel Stand	Red
4	3024.dat	Plate 1 x 1	Red
1	41769.dat	Wing 2 x 4 Right	Red
3	3710.dat	Plate 1 x 4	Red

Qty	Part	Description	Color
2	3665.dat	Slope Brick 45 2 x 1 Inverted	Red
1	41770.dat	Wing 2 x 4 Left	Red
1	3794.dat	Plate 1 x 2 with 1 Stud	Red
3	3666.dat	Plate 1 x 6	Red
2	4070.dat	Brick 1 x 1 with Headlight	Red
2	6091.dat	Brick 2 x 1 x 1 & 1/3 with Curved Top	Red
1	3795.dat	Plate 2 x 6	Red
2	3069b.dat	Tile 1 x 2 with Groove	Red
2	2436.dat	Bracket 1 x 2 - 1 x 4	Red
1	3020.dat	Plate 2 x 4	Red
2	50746.dat	Slope Brick 31 1 x 1 x 2/3	Red
4	30039.dat	Tile 1 x 1 with Groove	Red
2	6215.dat	Brick 2 x 3 with Curved Top	Red
4	2430.dat	Hinge Plate 1 x 4 Top	Red
2	4079.dat	Minifig Seat 2 x 2	Reddish Brown

Qty	Part	Description	Color
2	4073.dat	Plate 1 x 1 Round	Trans Yellow
1	44728.dat	Bracket 1 x 2 - 2 x 2	Dark Bluish Gray
1	3034.dat	Plate 2 x 8	Dark Bluish Gray
4	2412b.dat	Tile 1 x 2 Grille with Groove	Dark Bluish Gray
2	2444.dat	Plate 2 x 2 with Hole	Dark Bluish Gray
1	6636.dat	Tile 1 x 6	Black
2	87697.dat	Tyre 12/ 40 x 11 Wide with Center Band	Black
1	3828.dat	~Car Steering Wheel	Black
3	2412b.dat	Tile 1 x 2 Grille with Groove	Black
2	30648.dat	Tyre 24 x 14 with Shallow Staggered Treads	Black
2	3069b.dat	Tile 1 x 2 with Groove	Black
8	3062b.dat	Brick 1 x 1 Round with Hollow Stud	Light Bluish Gray
1	50943.dat	Car Engine 2 x 2 with Air Scoop	Light Bluish Gray
2	3022.dat	Plate 2 x 2	Light Bluish Gray
1	2431.dat	Tile 1 x 4 with Groove	Light Bluish Gray

Qty	Part	Description	Color
2	3023.dat	Plate 1 x 2	Light Bluish Gray
2	3673.dat	Technic Pin	Light Bluish Gray
2	6014.dat	Wheel Wide	Light Bluish Gray
1	3666.dat	Plate 1 x 6	Light Bluish Gray
2	55981.dat	Wheel 30.4 x 14 with Holes on Both Sides	Light Bluish Gray
4	6091.dat	Brick 2 x 1 x 1 & 1/3 with Curved Top	Light Bluish Gray
2	4488.dat	Plate 2 x 2 with Wheel Holder	Light Bluish Gray
4	48336.dat	Plate 1 x 2 with Handle Type 2	Light Bluish Gray
2	2412b.dat	Tile 1 x 2 Grille with Groove	Light Bluish Gray
1	4740.dat	Dish 2 x 2 Inverted	Light Bluish Gray
8	2555.dat	Tile 1 x 1 with Clip	Light Bluish Gray
3	3020.dat	Plate 2 x 4	Light Bluish Gray
2	4081b.dat	Plate 1 x 1 with Clip Light Type 2	Light Bluish Gray
4	4073.dat	Plate 1 x 1 Round	Light Bluish Gray

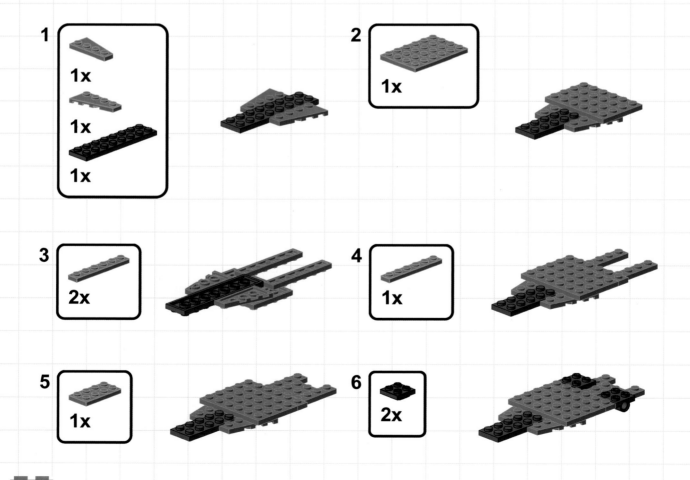

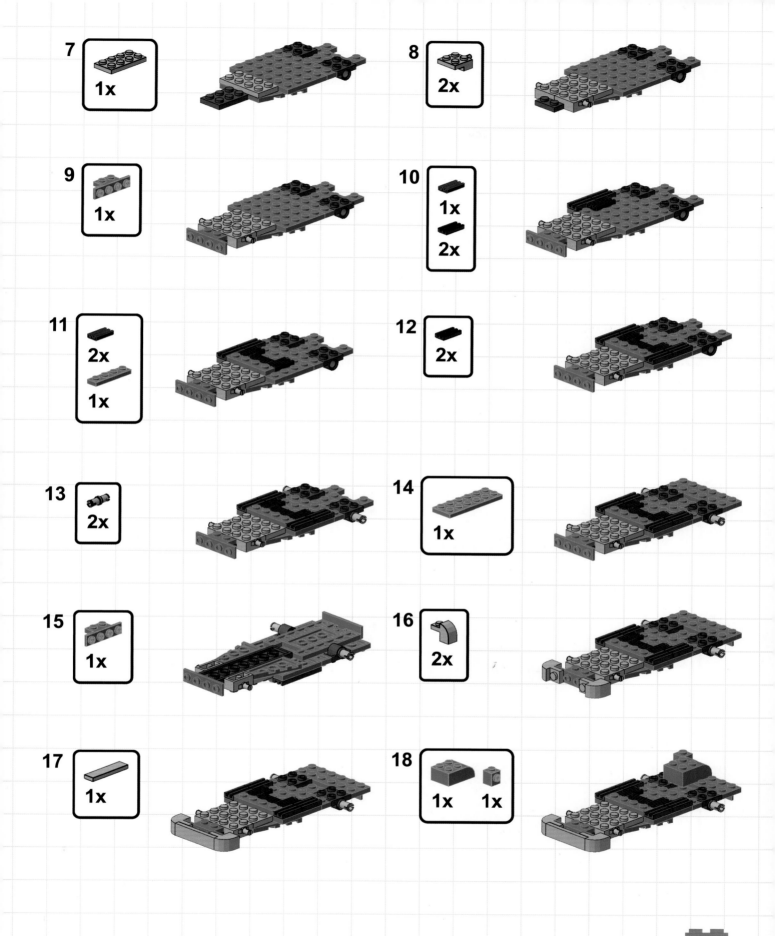

7 1x

8 2x

9 1x

10 1x 2x

11 2x 1x

12 2x

13 2x

14 1x

15 1x

16 2x

17 1x

18 1x 1x

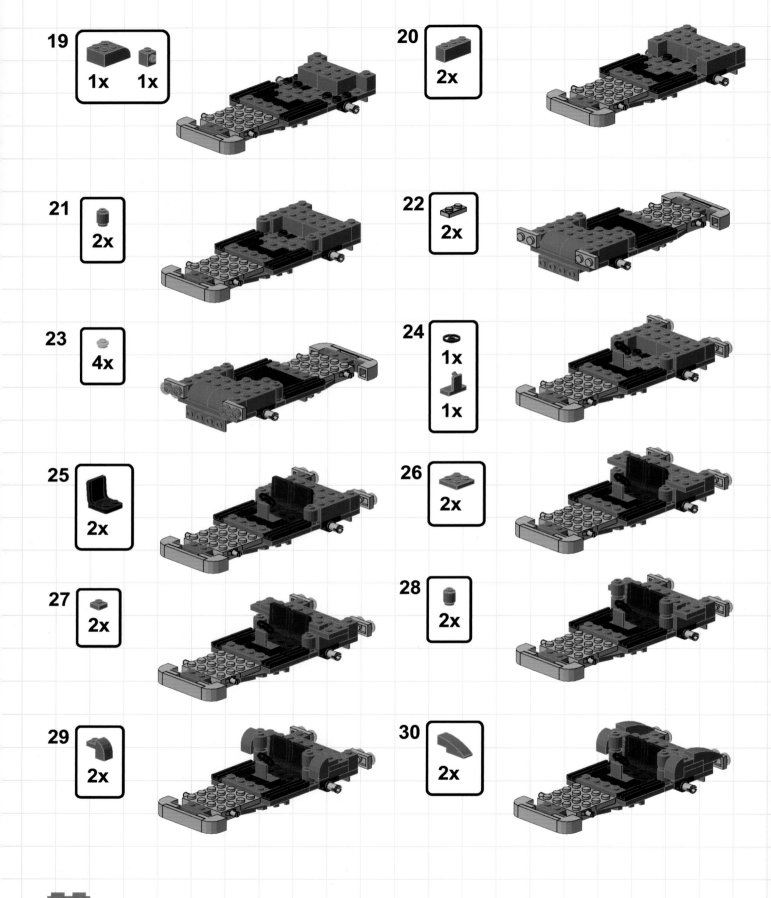

19 1x 1x

20 2x

21 2x

22 2x

23 4x

24 1x 1x

25 2x

26 2x

27 2x

28 2x

29 2x

30 2x

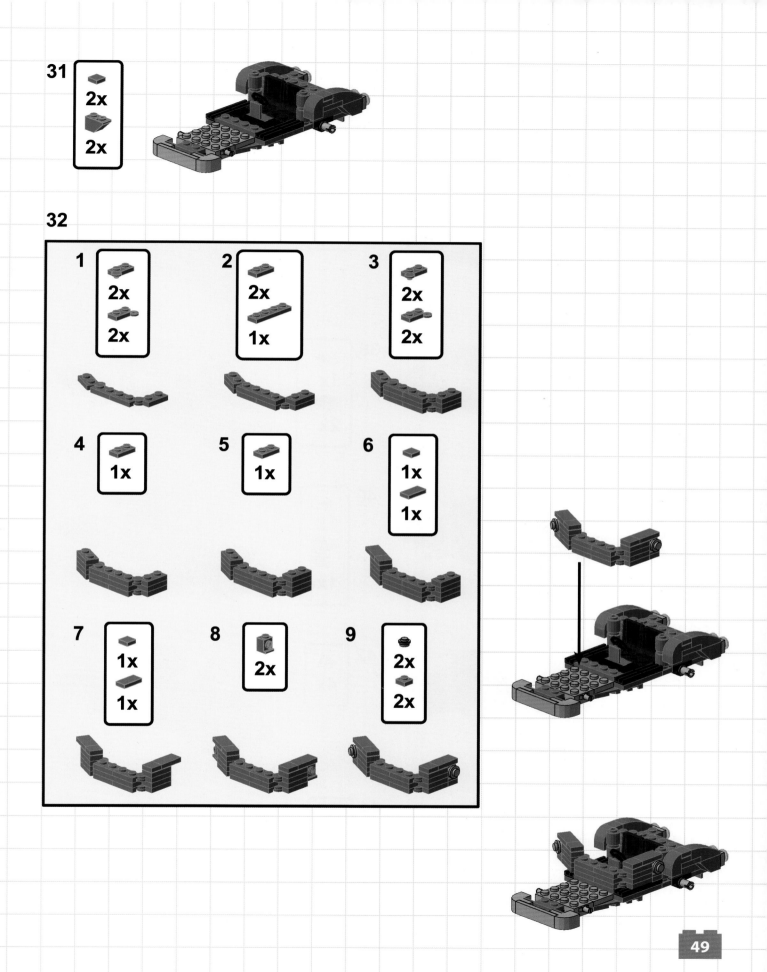

31
2x
2x

32

1 2x 2x

2 2x 1x

3 2x 2x

4 1x

5 1x

6 1x 1x

7 1x 1x

8 2x

9 2x 2x

33
1x
1x

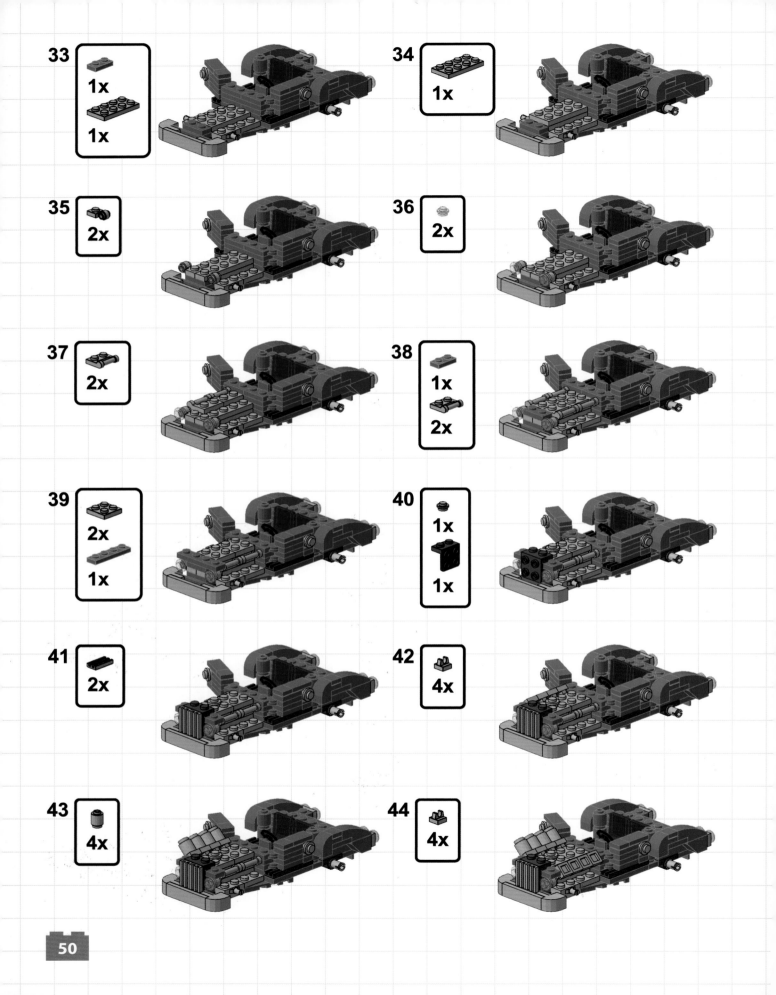

34
1x

35
2x

36
2x

37
2x

38
1x
2x

39
2x
1x

40
1x
1x

41
2x

42
4x

43
4x

44
4x

45 **4x**

46 **2x**

47 **1x** **1x**

48 **2x**

49 **1x** **1x**

50 **2x**

51 **1x** **1x**

52 **1x** **1x**

53 **2x** **2x**

54 **2x** **2x**

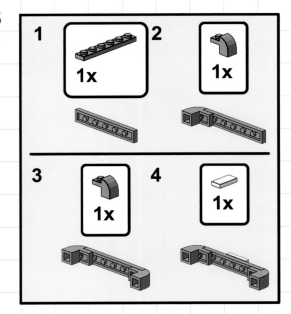

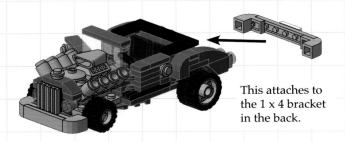

This attaches to the 1 x 4 bracket in the back.

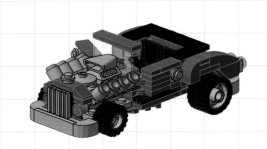

Bricks for Thought

What other parts allow SNOT *(Studs Not On Top)* building? Here's some bricks and brackets that will let you build sideways.

An oddball part is below — a 1 x 1 plate with Clip Light. This is the closest thing to a stud inverter in the LEGO element library. With it, you can build two different directions from the usual horizontal.

Space Fighter

Here's a model that is only a couple of years old, made from what was literally lying around on my work area—some call that "table scraps." I call them building doodles.

I just started building the nose, and the model sort of built itself. It can be built in different colors too, so make you own squadron!

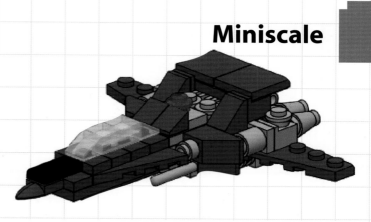

Qty	Part	Description	Color
1	4073.dat	Plate 1 x 1 Round	Trans Red
2	30039.dat	Tile 1 x 1 with Groove	Trans Yellow
2	50746.dat	Slope Brick 31 1 x 1 x 2/3	Trans Yellow
1	3023.dat	Plate 1 x 2	Trans Yellow
1	30244.dat	Tile 1 x 2 Grille with Groove	Dark Bluish Gray
1	3069b.dat	Tile 1 x 2 with Groove	Black
2	30244.dat	Tile 1 x 2 Grille with Groove	Light Bluish Gray
4	4081b.dat	Plate 1 x 1 with Clip Light Type 2	Light Bluish Gray
1	3839a.dat	Plate 1 x 2 with Handles Type 1	Light Bluish Gray
1	3794.dat	Plate 1 x 2 with 1 Stud	Light Bluish Gray
2	4070.dat	Brick 1 x 1 with Headlight	Light Bluish Gray
4	3062b.dat	Brick 1 x 1 Round with Hollow Stud	Light Bluish Gray
1	3020.dat	Plate 2 x 4	Light Bluish Gray

Qty	Part	Description	Color
2	2420.dat	Plate 2 x 2 Corner	Light Bluish Gray
2	3040b.dat	Slope Brick 45 2 x 1	Light Bluish Gray
8	4073.dat	Plate 1 x 1 Round	Light Bluish Gray
4	4589.dat	Cone 1 x 1	Light Bluish Gray
4	3023.dat	Plate 1 x 2	Light Bluish Gray
2	41770.dat	Wing 2 x 4 Left	Blue
7	3794.dat	Plate 1 x 2 with 1 Stud	Blue
2	4070.dat	Brick 1 x 1 with Headlight	Blue
1	3795.dat	Plate 2 x 6	Blue
1	3020.dat	Plate 2 x 4	Blue
1	49668.dat	Plate 1 x 1 with Tooth	Blue
2	41769.dat	Wing 2 x 4 Right	Blue
2	50746.dat	Slope Brick 31 1 x 1 x 2/3	Blue
2	3068b.dat	Tile 2 x 2 with Groove	Blue
6	3665.dat	Slope Brick 45 2 x 1 Inverted	Blue
2	3023.dat	Plate 1 x 2	Blue

Fuselage

1
1x

2
2x

3
2x

4
2x 2x

5
4x

6
1x 1x

7
2x 1x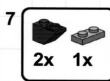

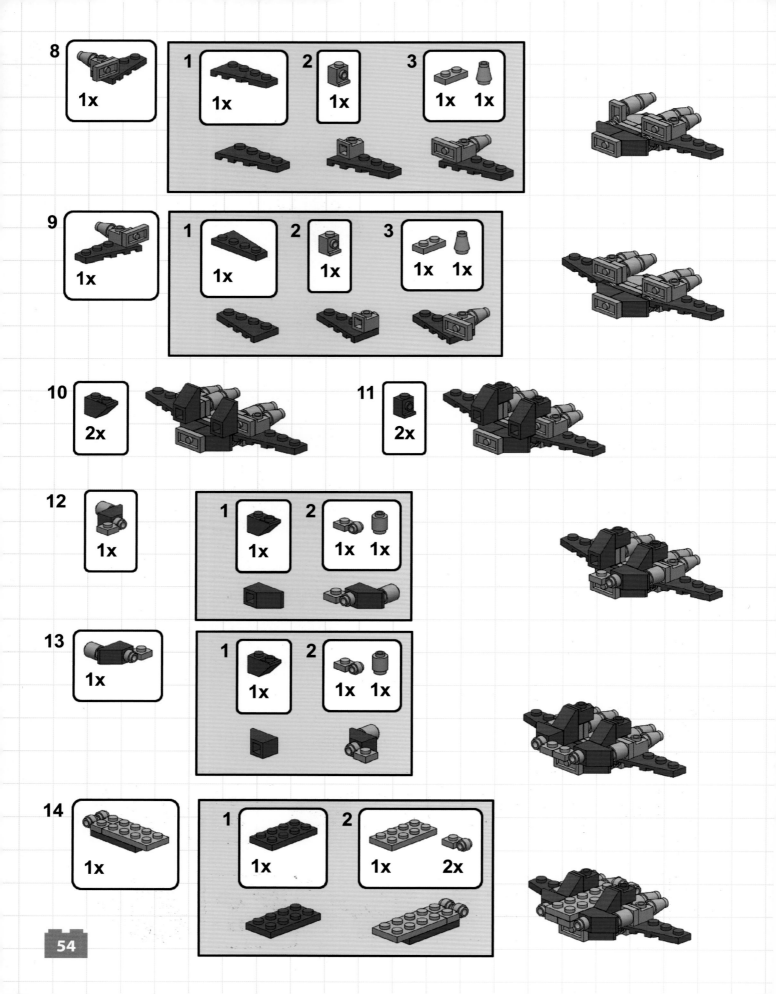

8 1x

1 1x **2** 1x **3** 1x 1x

9 1x

1 1x **2** 1x **3** 1x 1x

10 2x

11 2x

12 1x

1 1x **2** 1x 1x

13 1x

1 1x **2** 1x 1x

14 1x

1 1x **2** 1x 2x

15 1x 2x

16 4x

17
1 1x
2 1x
3 1x

Nose

1 1x

2 2x

3 1x

4 1x

5 1x 1x

6 4x

7 1x 1x

8 1x 2x

9 2x

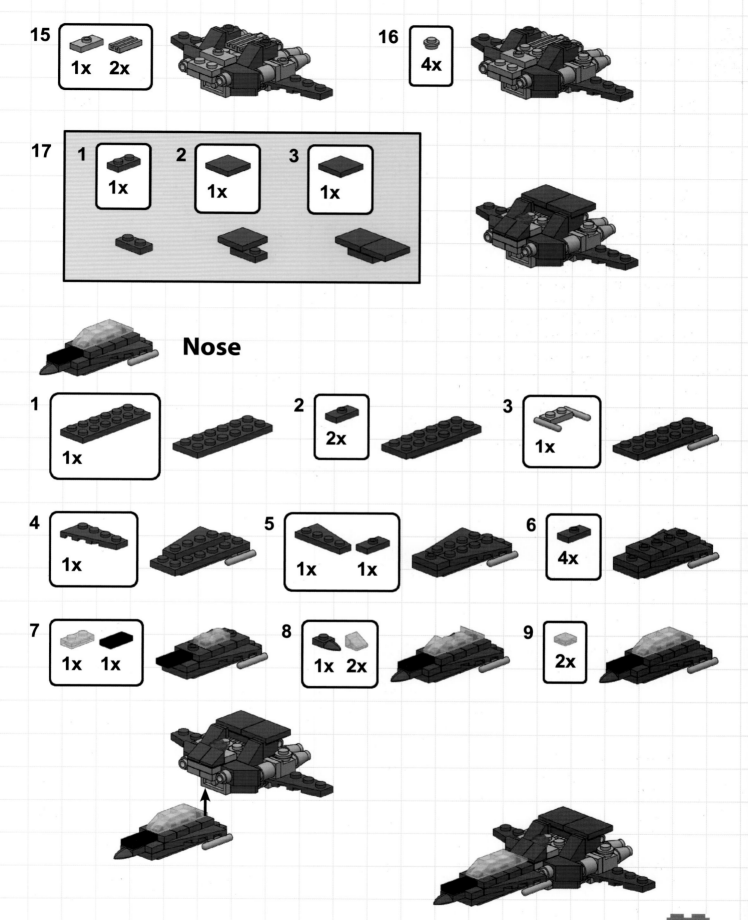

MINI Star Tours® Starspeeder 3000

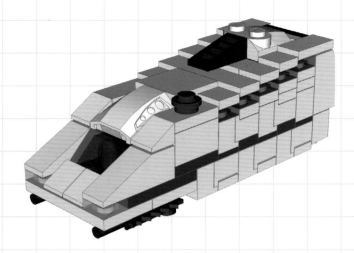

Design by Christopher Deck

Those of you who have visited one of the Disney theme parks probably will know "Star Tours," a simulator ride attraction based on the *Star Wars* Universe. The tour takes place in the well-known StarSpeeder 3000, the standard transport vessel of the Star Tours agency. Recently, the ride was refurbished with the Starspeeder 3000 replaced by the Starspeeder 1000. Here's a miniscale rendition of the classic ship.

The StarSpeeder 3000 basically looks like a simple trapezoid, but when you take a closer look, it will reveal some challenging details to build. The cockpit, for example, is embedded deeper in the sloped hull frame than the surface. There's five doors on each side, each of which has a small window on top. With each of the passenger doors, the height of the transport increases by one small step.

The version presented to you here features all these details with the accurate cockpit, weapons, astromech droid, maneuvering fin, detailed engine block, and a stepwise increase of the main body. Creating those five little steps was the toughest part while building this ship. With normal plate heights for each of the steps, it would have grown far too tall. Thus, there had to be half-plate heights for them, which resulted in a complicated construction for the rest of the model. It was a great feeling when everything turned out quite well.

Qty	Part	Description	Color
1	3039.dat	Slope Brick 45 2 x 2	Trans Black
1	3065.dat	Brick 1 x 2 without Centre Stud	Trans Black
13	3023.dat	Plate 1 x 2	Trans Black
6	3070b.dat	Tile 1 x 1 with Groove	White
2	3024.dat	Plate 1 x 1	White
1	41855.dat	Slope Brick Round 2 x 2 x 2/3	White
2	4286.dat	Slope Brick 33 3 x 1	White
1	44675.dat	Slope Brick Curved Top 2 x 2 x 1 with Dimples	White
4	2431.dat	Tile 1 x 4 with Groove	White
32	4070.dat	Brick 1 x 1 with Headlight	White
2	3794.dat	Plate 1 x 2 with 1 Stud	White
2	3020.dat	Plate 2 x 4	White
4	54200.dat	Slope Brick 31 1 x 1 x 2/3	White
2	2420.dat	Plate 2 x 2 Corner	White
2	60481.dat	Slope Brick 65 2 x 1 x 2	White
2	32000.dat	Technic Brick 1 x 2 with Holes	White

Qty	Part	Description	Color
4	6541.dat	Technic Brick 1 x 1 with Hole	White
1	54196.dat	Dish 2 x 2	White
1	3068b.dat	Tile 2 x 2 with Groove	White
4	3710.dat	Plate 1 x 4	White
3	3004.dat	Brick 1 x 2	White
3	3069b.dat	Tile 1 x 2 with Groove	White
4	3023.dat	Plate 1 x 2	White
2	3024.dat	Plate 1 x 1	Trans Yellow
4	50746.dat	Slope Brick 31 1 x 1 x 2/3	Trans Yellow
1	61409.dat	Slope Brick 18 2 x 1 x 2/3 Grille	Dark Bluish Gray
2	2412b.dat	Tile 1 x 2 Grille with Groove	Dark Bluish Gray
2	6117.dat	Minifig Tool Chainsaw Blade	Dark Bluish Gray
3	2436.dat	Bracket 1 x 2 - 1 x 4	Blue
4	3024.dat	Plate 1 x 1	Blue
2	3623.dat	Plate 1 x 3	Blue
2	2420.dat	Plate 2 x 2 Corner	Blue
1	6141.dat	Plate 1 x 1 Round	Blue

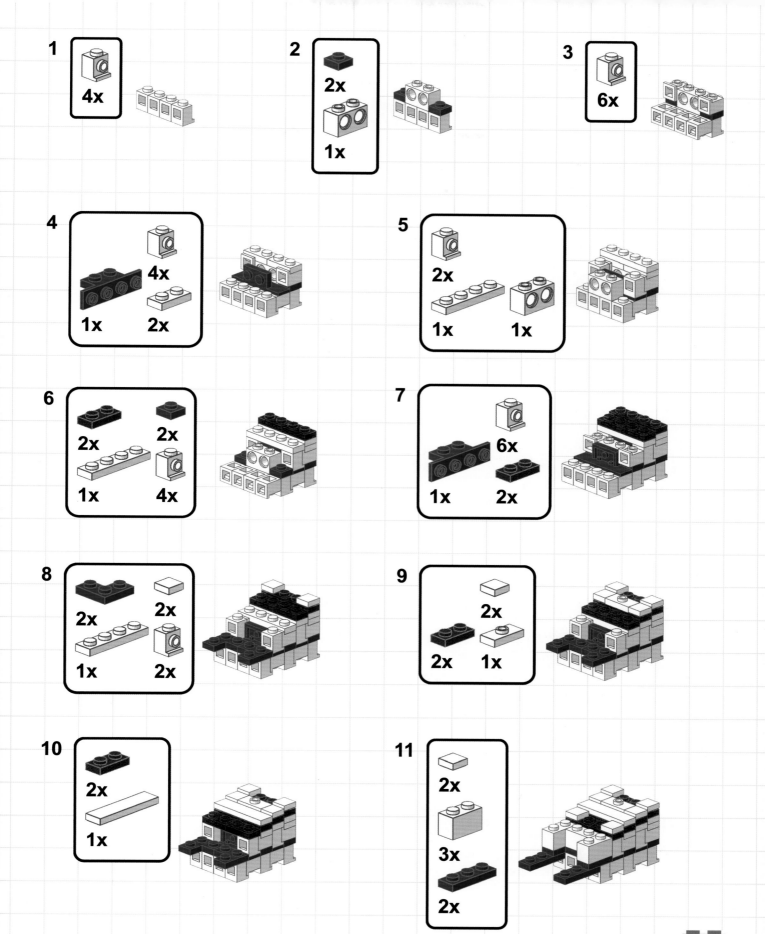

1 4x

2 2x 1x

3 6x

4 1x 4x 2x

5 2x 1x 1x

6 2x 2x 1x 4x

7 6x 1x 2x

8 2x 2x 1x 2x

9 2x 2x 1x

10 2x 1x

11 2x 3x 2x

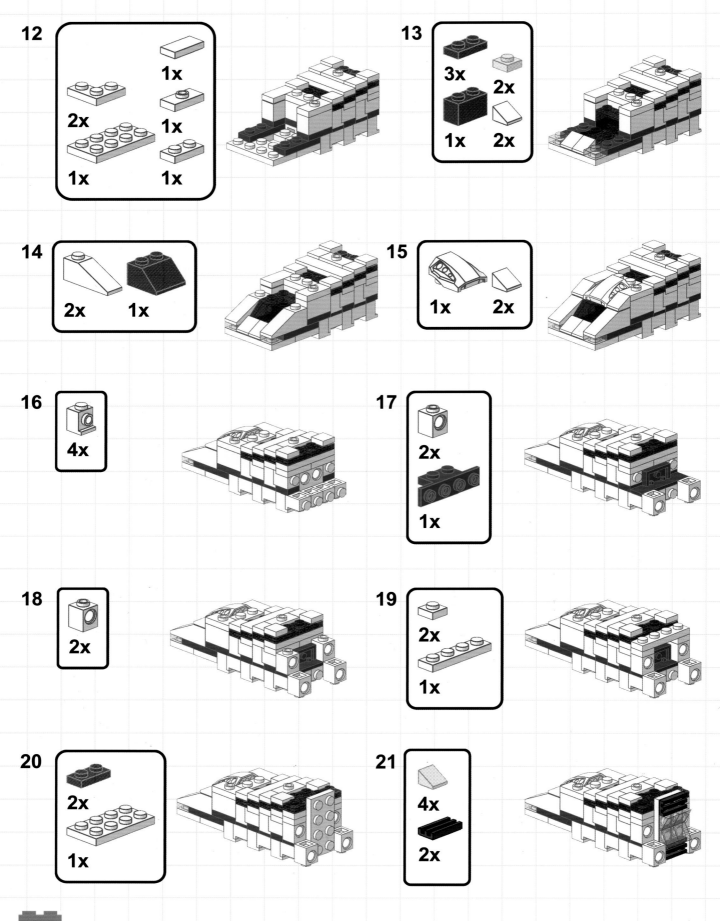

12 1x 2x 1x 1x 1x

13 3x 2x 1x 2x

14 2x 1x

15 1x 2x

16 4x

17 2x 1x

18 2x

19 2x 1x

20 2x 1x

21 4x 2x

22

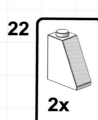

2x

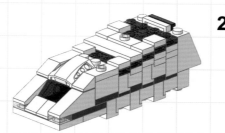

23

2x

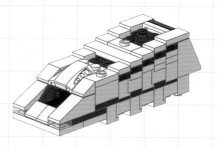

24

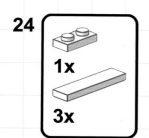

1x

3x

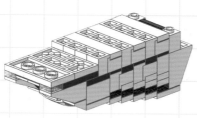

25

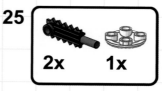

2x   **1x**

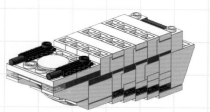

26

1x

1x

1x   **1x**

Bricks for Thought

Is there a ratio of plates to studs for building?

Yes. Two studs equals five plates in length, or more accurately, four plates and one tile on the top. A 2 x 2 box made of four plates and a tile is a cube. This cube can fit in a space 2 studs wide in a model. This can be multiplied to work out junction points.

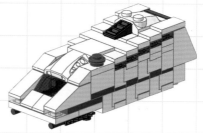

AH-64 Apache Longbow

This was one of my first microscale models. At the time, I was just exploring building at a small scale. I discovered that I really enjoy the problem-solving that has to be done to make such a small model. At this scale, details have to be minimized, so an object has to be distilled to its essence.

In this particular case, the shape of the helicopter is very distinct — it's not a particularly pretty look. However, the other element that stands out is the chain gun. This particular version of the Apache also has a radar mast, which is the ball on the rotor.

I posted this online in 2002, and feedback resulted in some changes to the engine to be more accurate. For the version here, I added some tiles to smooth the look of the Apache.

Qty	Part	Description	Color
2	3023.dat	Plate 1 x 2	Trans Black
1	30602.dat	Slope Brick Curved Top 2 x 2 x 1	Trans Black
2	6141.dat	Plate 1 x 1 Round	Dark Bluish Gray
1	6246a.dat	Minifig Tool Screwdriver	Dark Bluish Gray
4	3023.dat	Plate 1 x 2	Black
2	3623.dat	Plate 1 x 3	Black
4	3460.dat	Plate 1 x 8	Black
2	4032b.dat	Plate 2 x 2 Round with Axlehole Type 2	Black
4	3024.dat	Plate 1 x 1	Black
1	32474.dat	Technic Ball Joint	Black
1	3680c01.dat	Turntable 2 x 2 Plate (Complete)	Black
8	4073.dat	Plate 1 x 1 Round	Black
2	3062b.dat	Brick 1 x 1 Round with Hollow Stud	Light Bluish Gray
4	3022.dat	Plate 2 x 2	Light Bluish Gray
1	2431.dat	Tile 1 x 4 with Groove	Light Bluish Gray
2	3005.dat	Brick 1 x 1	Light Bluish Gray
1	3031.dat	Plate 4 x 4	Light Bluish Gray
2	6636.dat	Tile 1 x 6	Light Bluish Gray
2	42446.dat	Bracket 1 x 1 - 1 x 1	Light Bluish Gray

Qty	Part	Description	Color
4	3040b.dat	Slope Brick 45 2 x 1	Light Bluish Gray
7	3023.dat	Plate 1 x 2	Light Bluish Gray
2	3460.dat	Plate 1 x 8	Light Bluish Gray
3	3176.dat	Plate 3 x 2 with Hole	Light Bluish Gray
5	3024.dat	Plate 1 x 1	Light Bluish Gray
1	3665.dat	Slope Brick 45 2 x 1 Inverted	Light Bluish Gray
1	4274.dat	Technic Pin 1/2	Light Bluish Gray
4	3794.dat	Plate 1 x 2 with 1 Stud	Light Bluish Gray
5	3068b.dat	Tile 2 x 2 with Groove	Light Bluish Gray
5	4070.dat	Brick 1 x 1 with Headlight	Light Bluish Gray
1	2555.dat	Tile 1 x 1 with Clip	Light Bluish Gray
2	2420.dat	Plate 2 x 2 Corner	Light Bluish Gray
3	3069b.dat	Tile 1 x 2 with Groove	Light Bluish Gray
2	3020.dat	Plate 2 x 4	Light Bluish Gray
8	4081b.dat	Plate 1 x 1 with Clip Light Type 2	Light Bluish Gray
1	4286.dat	Slope Brick 33 3 x 1	Light Bluish Gray
2	3021.dat	Plate 2 x 3	Light Bluish Gray
5	4073.dat	Plate 1 x 1 Round	Light Bluish Gray
2	3004.dat	Brick 1 x 2	Light Bluish Gray

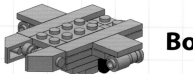

Body

1
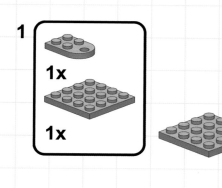 1x 1x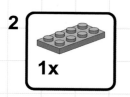

2
1x

3
2x

4
1x 1x 1x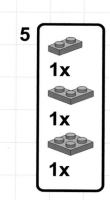

5
1x 1x 1x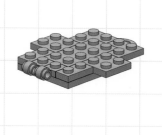

6
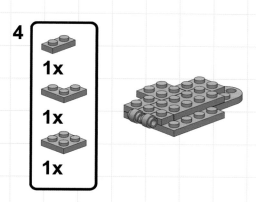
1 2x **2** 2x **3** 2x
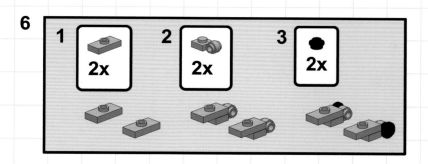
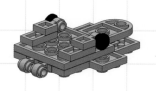

7
2x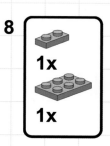

8
1x 1x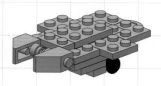

9

2x
2x

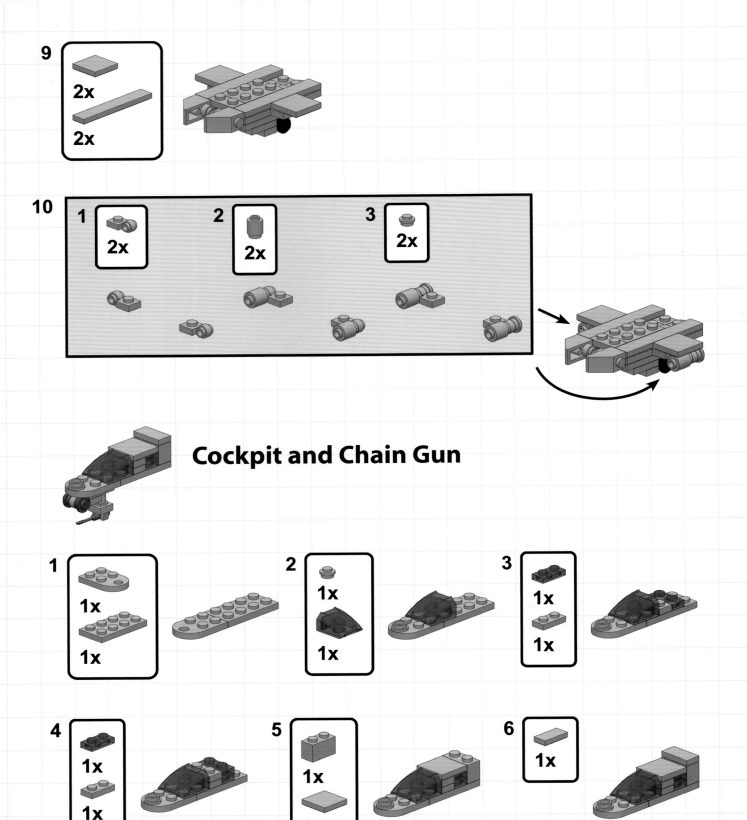

10

1 2x

2 2x

3 2x

Cockpit and Chain Gun

1 1x 1x

2 1x 1x

3 1x 1x

4 1x 1x

5 1x 1x

6 1x

7 1x

Insert on bottom
of plate, stud in tube

8 2x 1x

9 1 1x 2 1x 3 1x

The chain gun is not a
tight fit, so this can be
added later.

Tail

Insert on top
of plate, hole on stud

1 1x

2 1x

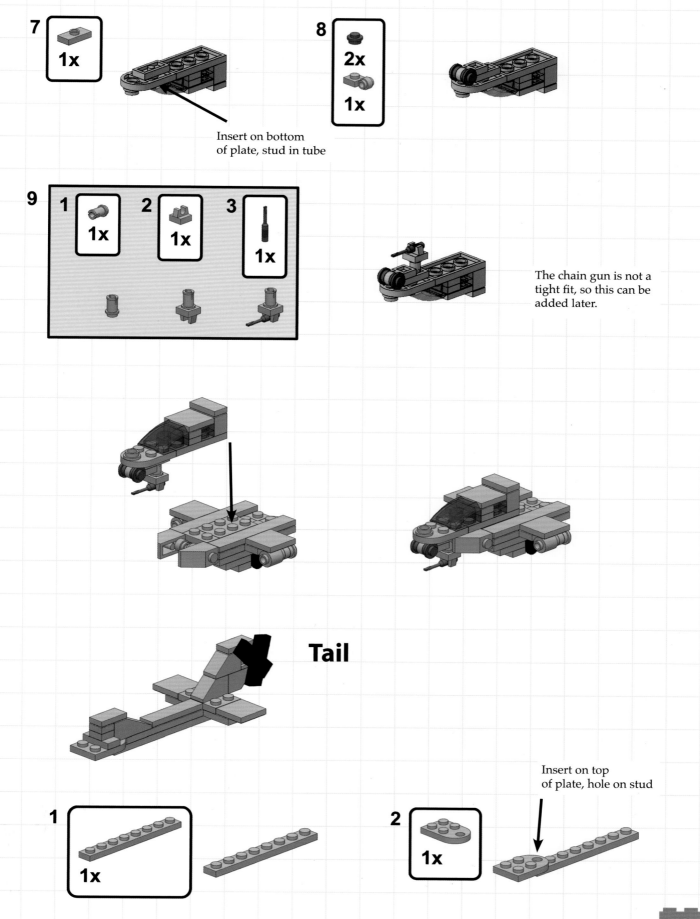

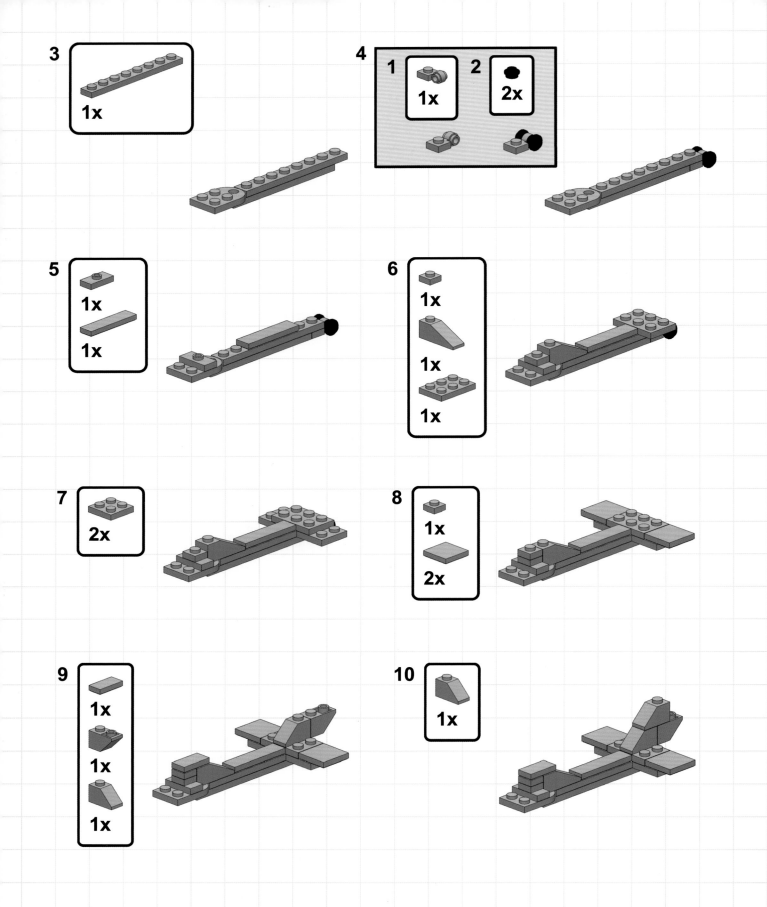

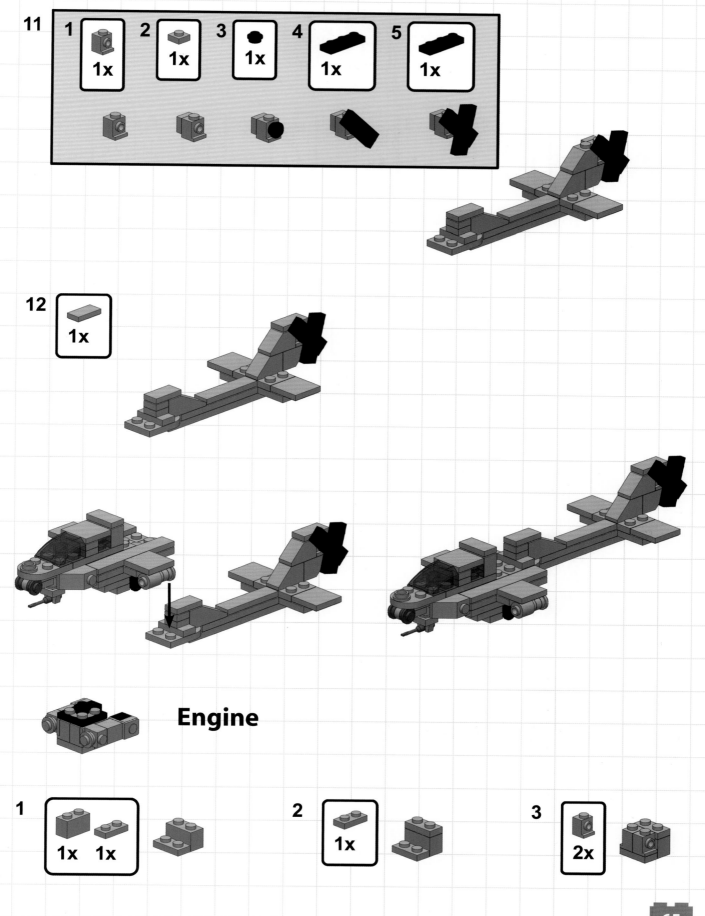

11

1 1x
2 1x
3 1x
4 1x
5 1x

12

1x

Engine

1
1x 1x

2
1x

3
2x

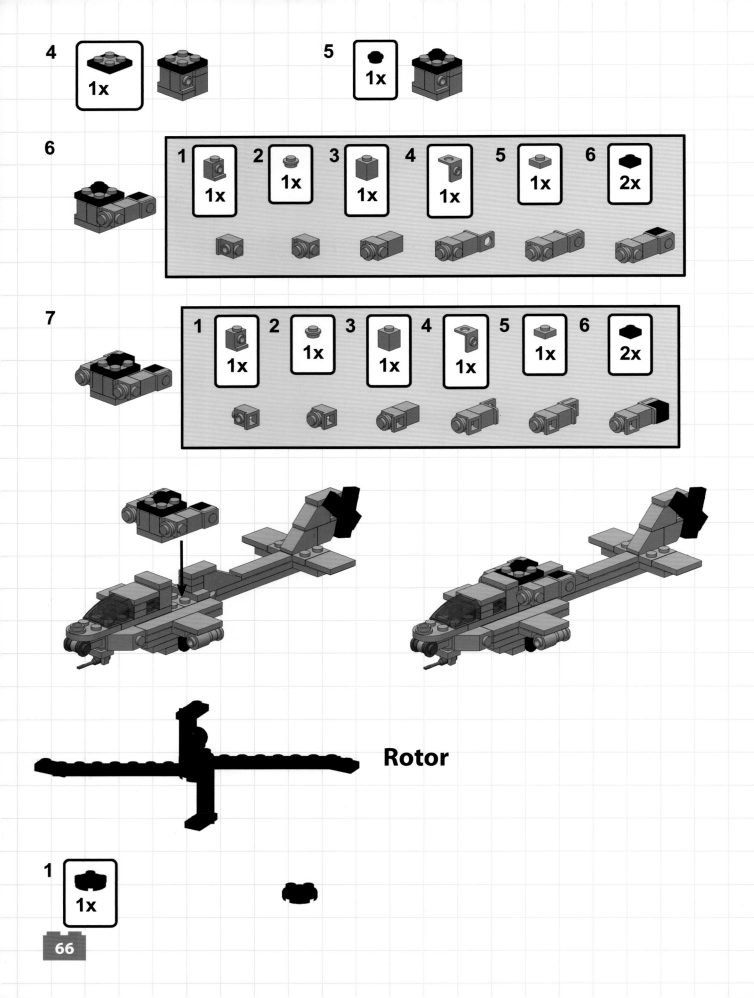

4 1x

5 1x

6
1. 1x
2. 1x
3. 1x
4. 1x
5. 1x
6. 2x

7
1. 1x
2. 1x
3. 1x
4. 1x
5. 1x
6. 2x

Rotor

1 1x

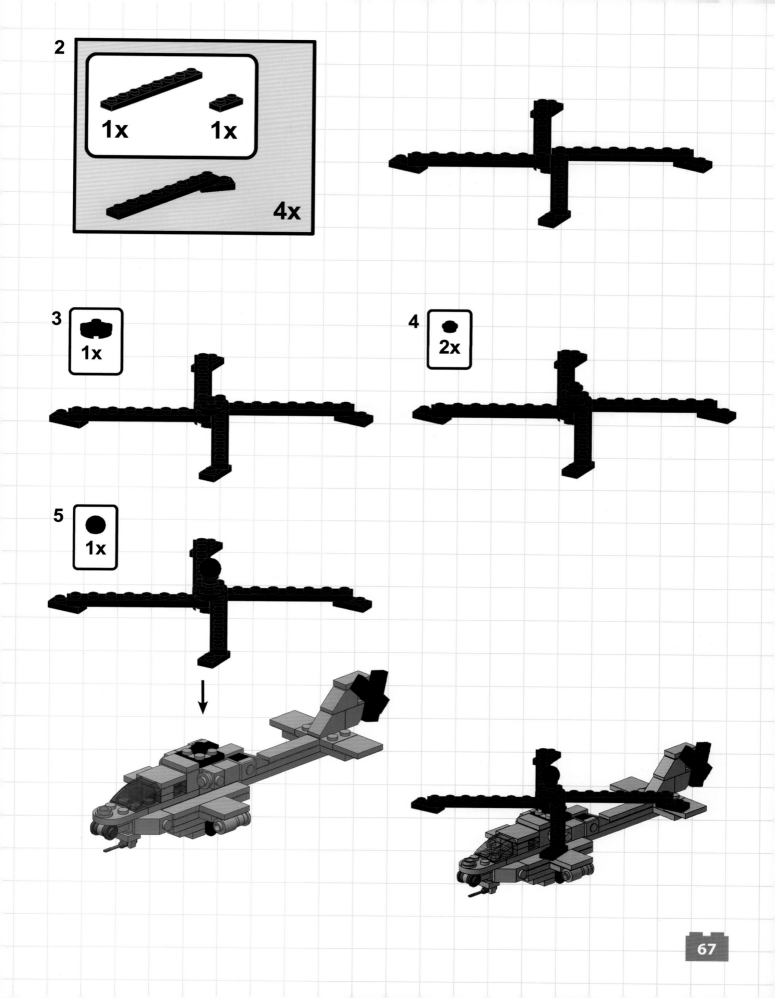

2

1x   1x

4x

3
1x

4
2x

5
1x

Miniscale

Pirate Ship

I always wanted to build a pirate ship, and once I began building microscale models, it was only logical to build a micro version. What is fun about this is that an entire pirate layout could be done on a blue baseplate, including islands and other ships.

The ship can also be modified to make different ships. You can lengthen it to add more guns and sails, or you can remove the cannons and build a sloop—your creativity is the only limit!

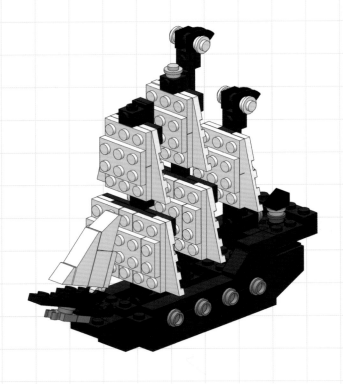

Qty	Part	Description	Color
1	54200.dat	Slope Brick 31 1 x 1 x 2/3	White
1	3040b.dat	Slope Brick 45 2 x 1	White
5	3023.dat	Plate 1 x 2	White
1	3623.dat	Plate 1 x 3	White
2	3710.dat	Plate 1 x 4	White
5	41769.dat	Wing 2 x 4 Right	White
5	41770.dat	Wing 2 x 4 Left	White
4	3020.dat	Plate 2 x 4	White
1	44301.dat	Hinge Plate 1 x 2 Locking with Single Finger on End Vertical	White
1	4286.dat	Slope Brick 33 3 x 1	White
11	3021.dat	Plate 2 x 3	White
4	4073.dat	Plate 1 x 1 Round	White
1	3004.dat	Brick 1 x 2	White
1	4073.dat	Plate 1 x 1 Round	Red
3	3031.dat	Plate 4 x 4	Brown
2	6636.dat	Tile 1 x 6	Brown
2	3040b.dat	Slope Brick 45 2 x 1	Brown
4	30010.dat	Panel 1 x 2 x 1	Brown
2	44302.dat	Hinge Plate 1 x 2 Locking with Dual Finger on End Vertical	Brown
1	4477.dat	Plate 1 x 10	Brown
8	3023.dat	Plate 1 x 2	Brown
11	3623.dat	Plate 1 x 3	Brown
1	3460.dat	Plate 1 x 8	Brown
3	3747a.dat	Slope Brick 33 3 x 2 Inverted without Ribs between Studs	Brown
6	3710.dat	Plate 1 x 4	Brown

Qty	Part	Description	Color
2	3665.dat	Slope Brick 45 2 x 1 Inverted	Brown
2	3024.dat	Plate 1 x 1	Brown
3	3794.dat	Plate 1 x 2 with 1 Stud	Brown
4	3666.dat	Plate 1 x 6	Brown
13	4070.dat	Brick 1 x 1 with Headlight	Brown
1	3010.dat	Brick 1 x 4	Brown
4	2420.dat	Plate 2 x 2 Corner	Brown
3	3069b.dat	Tile 1 x 2 with Groove	Brown
1	44567.dat	Hinge Plate 1 x 2 Locking with Single Finger On Side Vertical	Brown
2	3020.dat	Plate 2 x 4	Brown
2	4081b.dat	Plate 1 x 1 with Clip Light Type 2	Brown
1	3021.dat	Plate 2 x 3	Brown
4	3023.dat	Plate 1 x 2	Trans Yellow
2	4073.dat	Plate 1 x 1 Round	Yellow
9	6141.dat	Plate 1 x 1 Round	Light Bluish Gray
1	3024.dat	Plate 1 x 1	Light Bluish Gray
1	4085a.dat	Plate 1 x 1 with Clip Vertical Type 1	Light Bluish Gray
1	4073.dat	Plate 1 x 1 Round	Light Bluish Gray
1	54200.dat	Slope Brick 31 1 x 1 x 2/3	Black
1	3023.dat	Plate 1 x 2	Black
12	3024.dat	Plate 1 x 1	Black
4	49668.dat	Plate 1 x 1 with Tooth	Black
3	3069b.dat	Tile 1 x 2 with Groove	Black
1	4073.dat	Plate 1 x 1 Round	Black

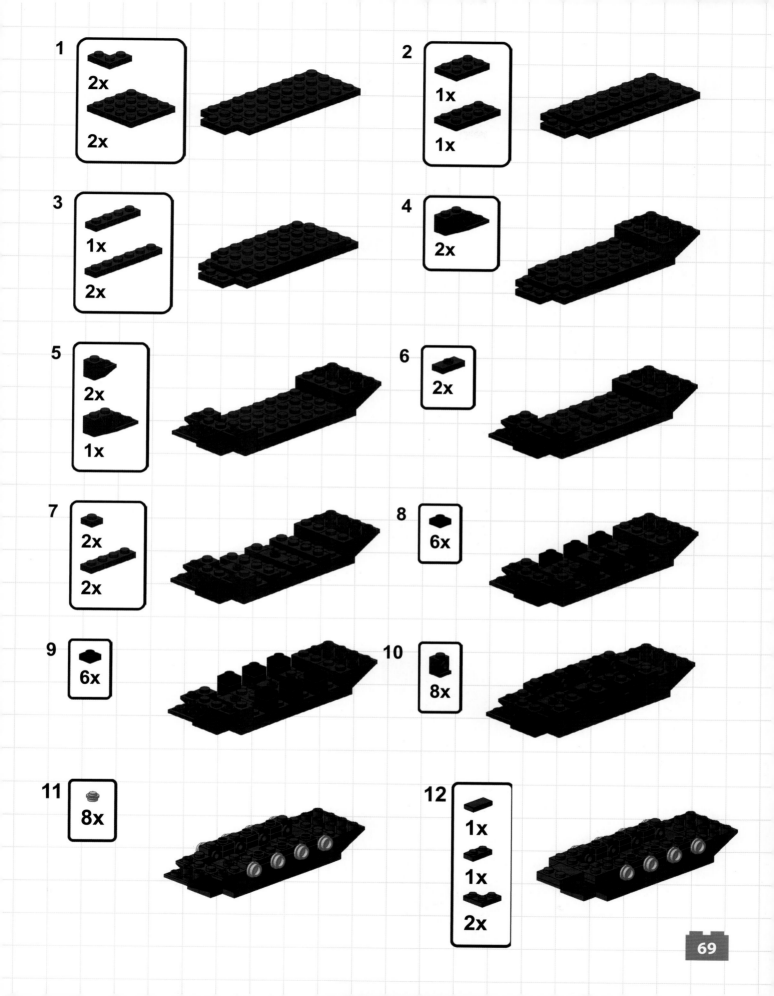

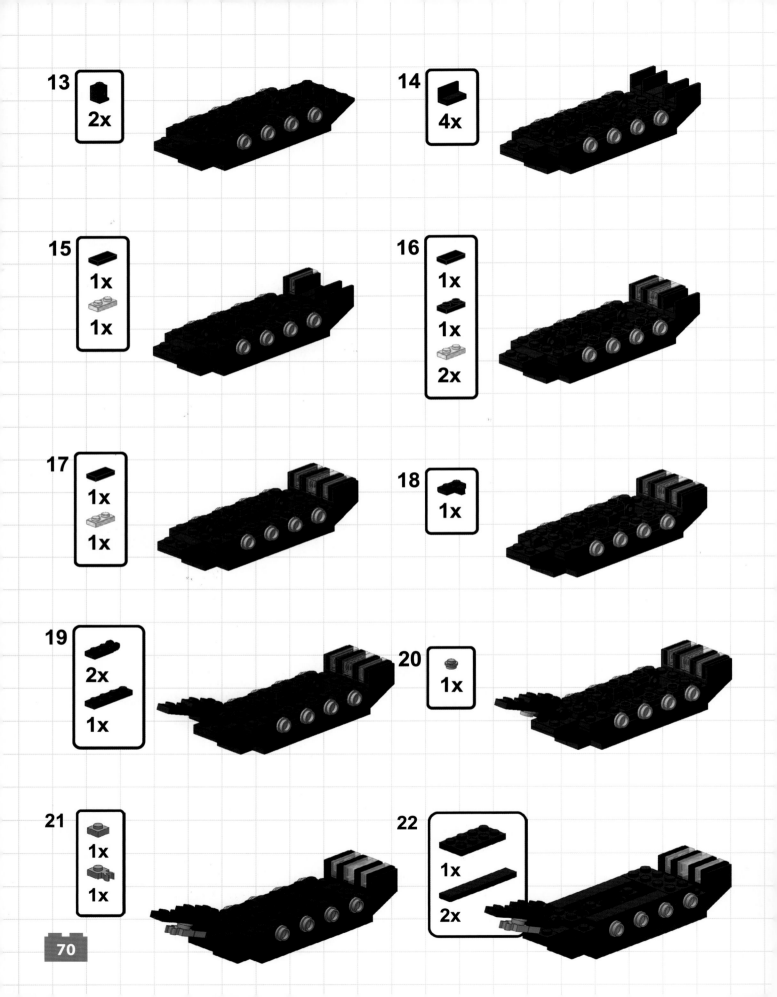

13 2x

14 4x

15 1x 1x

16 1x 1x 2x

17 1x 1x

18 1x

19 2x 1x

20 1x

21 1x 1x

22 1x 2x

23

1x

1x

24

1x

25

2x

1x

26

2x

1x

2x

1x

27

1x

1x

28

1x

1x

1x

1x

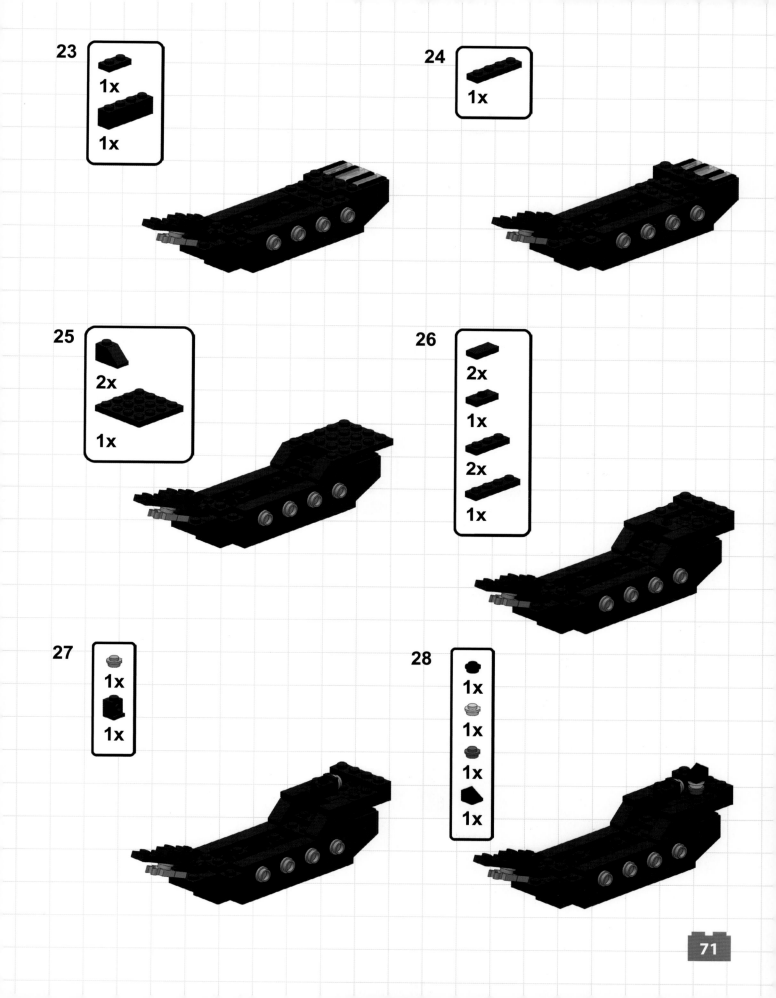

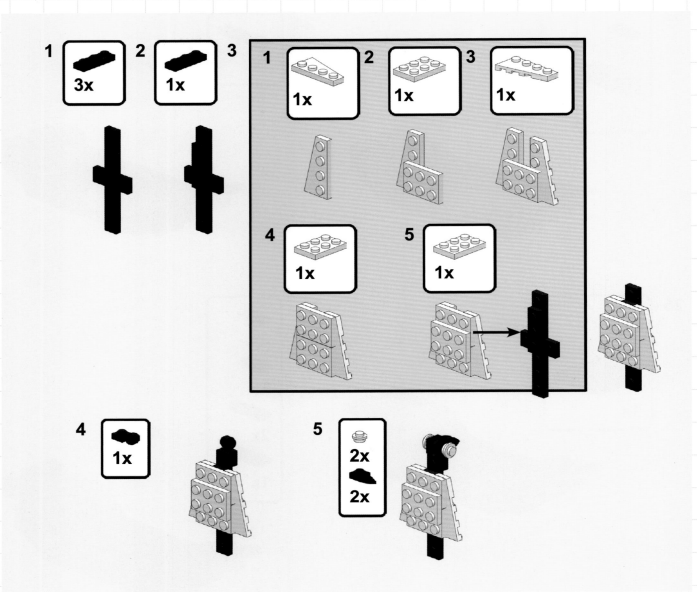

29

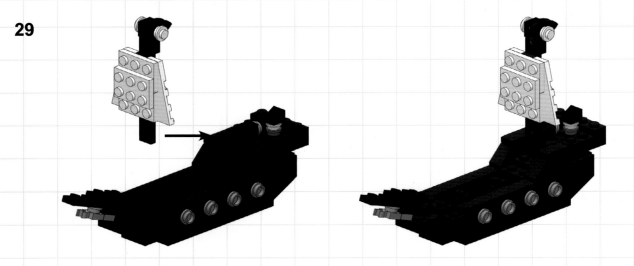

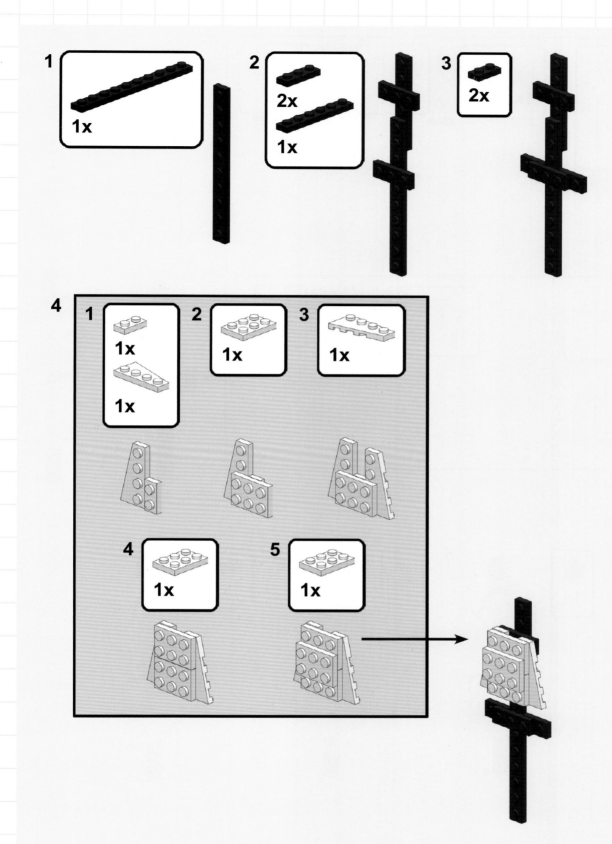

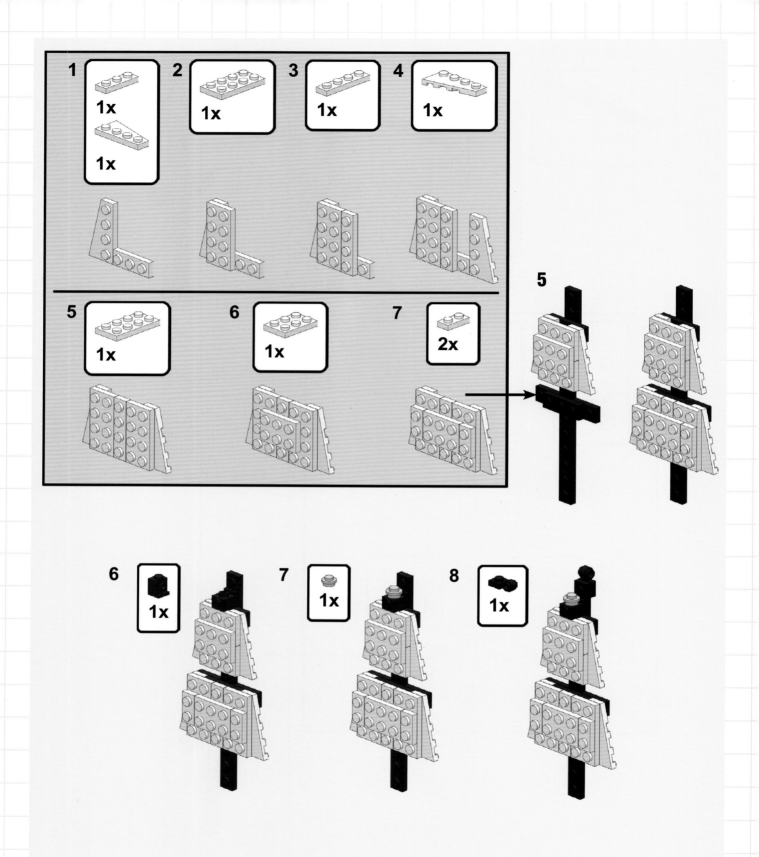

1 1x 1x

2 1x

3 1x

4 1x

5 1x

6 1x

7 2x

5

6 1x

7 1x

8 1x

9 **2x**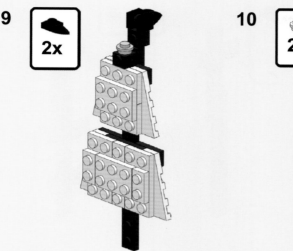

10 **2x**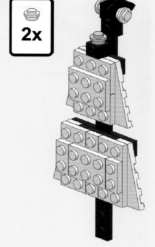

30

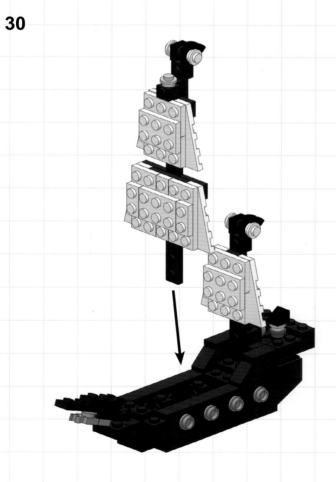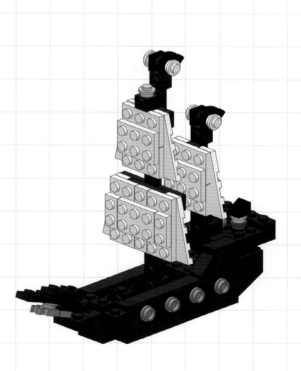

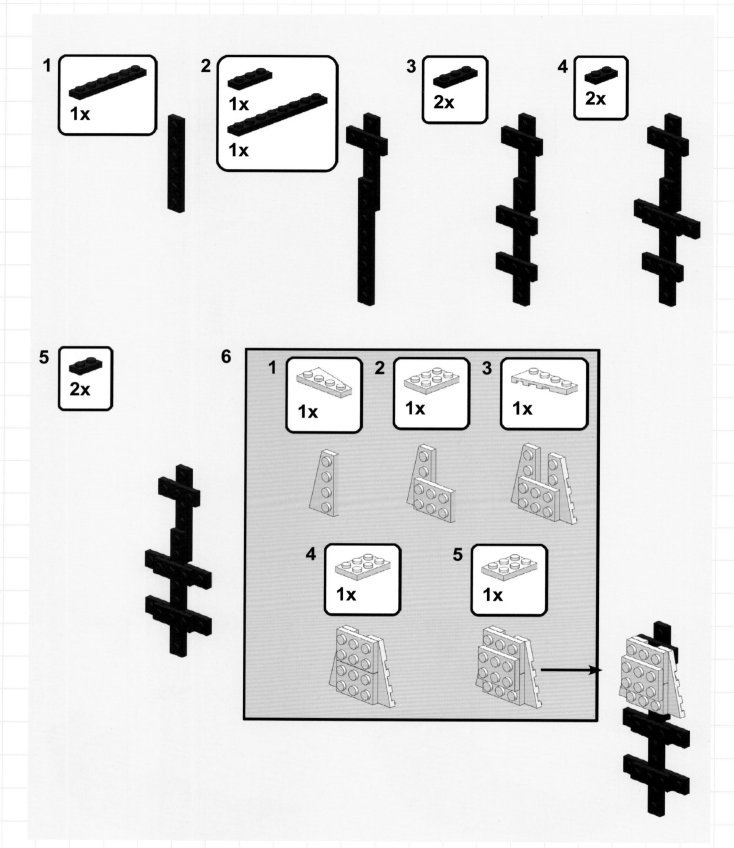

7

1 1x

2 1x

3 1x

4 1x

5 1x

6 1x

7 2x

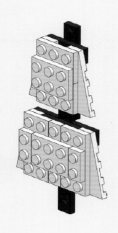

8 1x

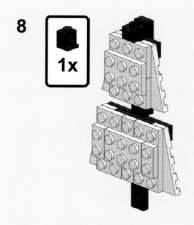

31

32

Ready to take your building to the next level?

Download a FREE BONUS SET OF FIGHTER JET INSTRUCTIONS now!

As a special bonus for purchasers of this book, you can download a **FREE BONUS SET OF INSTRUCTIONS** to build a Fighter Jet at this link:

http://www.twomorrows.com/media/FighterJet.pdf

This jet has working landing gear, a canopy that opens, and moving wing flaps. These detailed instructions were too lengthy to print here, but you can download them now, and enjoy building this more extensive set. Then, look for more advanced instructions in *You Can Build It, Book 2*, coming soon at *www.twomorrows.com*!

Brick Journal
people • building • community

THE MAGAZINE FOR LEGO® ENTHUSIASTS OF ALL AGES!

BRICKJOURNAL magazine (edited by Joe Meno) spotlights all aspects of the **LEGO®** Community, showcasing events, people, and models every issue, with contributions and how-to articles by top builders worldwide, new product intros, and more. Available in both **FULL-COLOR** print and digital editions. Print subscribers get the digital version **FREE!**

DIGITAL EDITIONS AVAILABLE FOR ONLY $3.95

LEGO, the Minifigure, and the Brick and Knob configurations are trademarks of the LEGO Group of Companies.

BRICKJOURNAL #1
The ultimate resource for **LEGO** enthusiasts of all ages, showcasing events, people, and models! **FULL-COLOR** #1 features an interview with Certified LEGO Professional **NATHAN SAWAYA**, car designs by **STEPHAN SANDER**, step-by-step building instructions and techniques for all skill levels, new set reviews, on-the-scene reports from **LEGO** community events, and other surprises!

(84-page print magazine) **SOLD OUT**
(Digital Edition) **$3.95**

BRICKJOURNAL #2
This **FULL-COLOR** issue spotlights blockbuster summer movies, LEGO style! Go behind the scenes for new sets for **INDIANA JONES**, and see new models, including an **MINI FLYING WING** and a **LEGO CITY**, a lifesize **IRON MAN**, plus how to **CUSTOMIZE MINIFIGURES**, **BUILDING INSTRUCTIONS**, a tour of the **ONLINE LEGO FACTORY**, and lots more!

(84-page **FULL-COLOR** magazine) **$8.95**
(Digital Edition) **$3.95**

BRICKJOURNAL #3
Event Reports from **BRICKWORLD**, **FIRST LEGO LEAGUE WORLD FESTIVAL** and **PIECE OF PEACE** (Japan), spotlight on our cover model builder **BRYCE McGLONE**, behind the scenes of **LEGO BATMAN**, **LEGO** at **COMIC-CON INTERNATIONAL**, **FIRST LEGO LEAGUE WORLD FESTIVAL**, plus **STEP-BY-STEP BUILDING INSTRUCTIONS, TECHNIQUES**, and more!

(84-page **FULL-COLOR** magazine) **$8.95**
(Digital Edition) **$3.95**

BRICKJOURNAL #4
Interviews with **LEGO BUILDERS** including cover model builder **ARTHUR GUGICK**, event reports from **BRICKFAIR** and others, touring the **LEGO IDEA HOUSE**, plus **STEP-BY-STEP BUILDING INSTRUCTIONS** and **TECHNIQUES** for all skill levels, **NEW SET REVIEWS**, and an extensive report on constructing the Chinese Olympic Village in **LEGO!**

(84-page **FULL-COLOR** magazine) **$8.95**
(Digital Edition) **$3.95**

BRICKJOURNAL #5
Event report on the **MINDSTORMS 10th ANNIVERSARY** at **LEGO HEADQUARTERS**, Pixar's **ANGUS MACLANE** on LEGO in film-making, a glimpse at the LEGO Group's past with the **DIRECTOR OF LEGO'S IDEA HOUSE**, event reports, a look at how **SEAN KENNEY's** LEGO creations ended up on **NBC'S 30 ROCK** television show, instructions and spotlights on builders, and more!

(84-page **FULL-COLOR** magazine) **$8.95**
(Digital Edition) **$3.95**

BRICKJOURNAL #6
Spotlight on **CLASSIC SPACE SETS** and a look at new ones, **BRANDON GRIFFITH** shows his **STAR TREK MODELS**, LEGO set designers discuss their work creating the **SPACE POLICE** with **PIRATE SETS**, **POWER FUNCTIONS TRAIN DEVELOPMENT**, the world's **TALLEST LEGO TOWER**, **MINI-FIGURE CUSTOMIZATION**, plus coverage of **BRICKFEST 2009** and more!

(84-page **FULL-COLOR** magazine) **$8.95**
(Digital Edition) **$3.95**

BRICKJOURNAL #7
Focuses on the new **LEGO ARCHITECTURE** line, with a look at the new sets designed by **ADAM REED TUCKER**, plus interviews with other architectural builders, including **SPENCER REZKALLA**. Also, behind the scenes on the creation of **POWER MINERS** and the **GRAND CAROUSEL**, a **LEGO BATTLESHIP** over 20 feet long, reports from LEGO events worldwide, and more!

(84-page **FULL-COLOR** magazine) **$8.95**
(Digital Edition) **$3.95**

BRICKJOURNAL #8
We go to the Middle Ages, with a look at the LEGO Group's **CASTLE LINE**, featuring an interview with the designer behind the first LEGO castle set, the **YELLOW CASTLE**. Also: we spotlight builders that have created their own large-scale version of the castle, and interview other castle builders, plus a report on **BRICKWORLD** in Chicago, ands still more instructions and building tips!

(84-page **FULL-COLOR** magazine) **$8.95**
(Digital Edition) **$3.95**

BRICKJOURNAL #9
BrickJournal looks at **LEGO® DISNEY SETS**, with features on the Disney LEGO sets of the past (**MICKEY** and **MINNIE**) and present (**TOY STORY** and **PRINCE OF PERSIA**)! We also present Disney models built by LEGO fans, and a look at the newest Master Build model at **WALT DISNEY WORLD**, plus articles and instructions on building and customization, and more!

(84-page **FULL-COLOR** magazine) **$8.95**
(Digital Edition) **$3.95**

BRICKJOURNAL #10
BrickJournal goes undersea with looks at the creation of LEGO's new **ATLANTIS SETS**, plus a spotlight on a fan-created underwater theme, **THE SEA MONKEYS**, with builder **FELIX GRECO!** Also, a report on the **LEGO WORLD** convention in the Netherlands, **BUILDER SPOTLIGHTS**, **INSTRUCTIONS** and ways to **CUSTOMIZE MINIFIGURES, LEGO HISTORY**, and more!

(84-page **FULL-COLOR** magazine) **$8.95**
(Digital Edition) **$3.95**

BRICKJOURNAL #11
"Racers" theme issue, with building tips on race cars by the **ARVO BROTHERS**, interview with **LEGO RACERS** designer **ANDREW WOODMAN**, **LEGO FORMULA ONE RACING**, **TECHNIC SPORTS CAR** building, event reports, instructions and columns on **MINIFIGURE CUSTOMIZATION** and **MICRO BUILDING**, builder spotlights, **LEGO HISTORY**, and more!

(84-page **FULL-COLOR** magazine) **$8.95**
(Digital Edition) **$3.95**

BRICKJOURNAL #12
A look at school sculptures by **NATHAN SAWAYA**, builder **MARCOS BESSA's** creations, **ANGUS MACLANE's** CubeDudes, a Nepali Diorama by **JORDAN SCHWARTZ**, instructions to build a school bus for your LEGO town, minifigure customizations, how a **POWER MINERS** model became one for **ATLANTIS**, building standards, and much more!

(84-page **FULL-COLOR** magazine) **$8.95**
(Digital Edition) **$3.95**

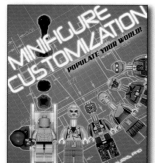
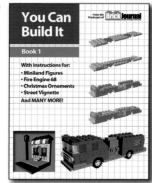
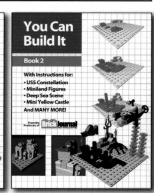